Cash management . . .
on a Shoestring

Cash management . . . on a Shoestring

Tony Dalton

A & C Black • London

First published in Great Britain 2007

A & C Black Publishers Ltd
38 Soho Square, London W1D 3HB

British Library Cataloguing in Publication Data
A CIP record for this book is available from the British Library.

ISBN: 978-0-7136-7706-5

This book is produced using paper that is made from wood grown in managed, sustainable forests. It is natural, renewable and recyclable. The logging and manufacturing processes conform to the environmental regulations of the country of origin.

Design by Fiona Pike, Pike Design, Winchester
Typeset by RefineCatch Limited, Bungay, Suffolk
Printed in Italy by Rotolito

CONTENTS

CONTENTS

FOREWORD

Have you ever looked at a growing pile of invoices you can't pay and felt the panic mount? I have. Money worries affect all small business owners at one time or another. The pressure to cope is intense, and dealing with financial difficulties can leave you feeling isolated. There is a lot you can do to help yourself, though, even when things seem at their bleakest, and reading this book is an excellent first step. It will help you to cope with many of the financial challenges business life throws at us, using proven techniques to help you manage your cash more effectively and get the results you want.

The information/reality gap

There's no real way to learn how to run a business other than getting out there and doing it. Yes, Business Link and other organisations run courses to help you with the nuts and bolts of setting up, but beyond that, you're pretty much on your own. Other establishments and consultants offer relevant-sounding training, but not all of them are based on first-hand experience of running a small business. If you've never had to worry about when the money's coming in yourself, it's hard to offer relevant coping strategies to people who *do* need to worry about it.

When you were preparing to start your own business, you should have worked out a simple cash plan that showed how much money you needed each month to cover expenses, as well as how much you expected to get in each month, in order to be confident of actually making some money. Armed with these figures, you go to the bank, borrow the money – usually on an overdraft secured against your house – and off you go. This is when reality strikes: you find out that things don't always go to plan and it can then seem as though you're stumbling from one cash crisis to the next.

I've been there too, but having run several businesses – and made many of the classic cash-management mistakes along the way – I feel that I am slowly beginning to learn how to survive in the small business jungle.

When I set up my first company, I left the vast conglomerate of Unilever, confident that I knew all about business and that all those management courses they had sent me on were all the training I needed. I was confident. I went out on my own and started a small business. I was hit by a cash-flow crisis.

I hadn't expected this and couldn't find any books to help me sort it out. Which is how I got here. My aim in writing this book is to show you that if you look at your business purely from a cash basis, concentrating on getting the money in and controlling the flow of cash through it, you will make profits. Most important of all, though, you'll be able to concentrate on the business rather than on the bank manager. The techniques have proved so successful for me that I now act as a consultant for small businesses in financial crisis. I call these tactics you're going to read about 'think cash'.

Let's get started.

1 INTRODUCTION

According to a survey conducted in 2005 by Bank of Scotland Corporate Banking, almost two-thirds of all small businesses admitted they had paid the same invoice *twice*. This adds up to a staggering £2.8 billion! Eddie Morrison, Managing Director of BOS Corporate Banking, explained that this was mainly due to simple errors arising from cash management being way down the list of most small companies' priorities.

Eddie Morrison is absolutely right. When you run a small business, you're working so hard that you simply don't have the time to cover all aspects as thoroughly as you would like. It is hardly surprising that you don't have the time to watch your cash flow. That is, of course, until you don't have the money to pay your bills. That's when you need to think cash.

Living in Monaco is a man who puts cash at the top of his list. He holds the record for turning a company around from suffering a minus valuation to being worth over £1 billion in the shortest time. His name is Philip Green. In 2000, he bought an under-performing retail chain, BHS, and within a year declared profits of over £100 million, making himself a billionaire in the process. Just a year later, he bought another company, Arcadia. You may not have heard of it, but you will doubtless have heard of some of the High Street names it owns, which include Dorothy Perkins, Topshop, Miss Selfridge and Burton. Within two years, Green announced a 95.8% increase in operating profit and reported that he had repaid all the loans he took out to buy it.

Quite a businessman, and yet one not in the good books of the City investment trusts and pension companies. Why? Because he doesn't make money for them, he makes it for himself! On the other hand, the banks that lend him money love him. He is a good risk who repays them quickly so they make money safely, and all banks like that.

Wouldn't it be great to be loved by the banks? Especially if they kept offering you money when you didn't need it? So, what is his secret? What makes him so special that he can make all this money? He is very open about it, and it isn't rocket science. It is, however, good cash management. Basically, if you manage the flow of money and the creation of cash, profits will follow. Remember: a profitable company *can* go bust while one with a positive cash flow won't.

Here's another illustration from the High Street. In 1986, David Jones was chief executive of a mail order house, Grattan, which merged with the fashion chain Next. Next was one of the retailing sensations of the decade. It had been created by the charismatic George Davies, who at that time was still chief executive. After the Grattan merger, David Jones became Davies's deputy. Unfortunately, once he had taken up his new position, he found that over an 18-month period, Next had declared profits of £100 million to satisfy the stock market, but even with these perceived profits it had an actual cash outflow of £250 million! David Jones knew this couldn't continue, because if it did, Next would inevitably go bust. This led to a highly public boardroom clash, resulting in the departure of George Davies. Jones took over and turned the company around by putting cash management first.

Once you start thinking like David Jones did, you'll look at your business differently and eventually you'll be able to stop worrying about those time-wasting calls from the bank manager. Why? Because there simply won't be any and you'll only use the bank for cheque processing. You won't need an overdraft, either. Freeing yourself up from these worries will give you time to work on letting your business make money.

'Think cash' is management *practice*, not management theory. It's a proven method of running a successful business. It's about going back to basics, and in essence it's very simple. It revolves around:

- getting your money in quicker
- making better use of that money when you get it
- not paying it out too quickly

Whatever size of budget you manage, these principles are key. For example, some years ago, John Madejski, the multi-millionaire former owner of *Auto Trader* and owner of Reading Football Club, took part in a television documentary, which saw him swap lives for one week with a single mother who subsisted on benefits. First, the single mother stayed at his vast mansion with her children for a week, which everyone enjoyed. The really interesting bit, though, came when he went to stay with her for a week. It was a revelation to him that she was an accomplished cash manager, surviving on a very limited weekly income and managing it sensibly.

She knew how much money was coming in each week, but she also knew that each week she would need to spend more. Life had taught her that it was only by clever cash management that she would solve the problem of finding enough money to feed her children. How did she do this?

She couldn't increase her income as jobs weren't readily available, and even if she found one, it would mean that she would have to leave her children with someone else and her additional income would end up paying for a childminder. So she looked at her expenses and discovered the cash savings that would enable her to feed her children, and feed them well, while staying within her budget. Each night she knew exactly at which supermarket and at what time they would be cutting the prices of their fresh food, and she was able to feed her children on it at a fraction of the cost that John Madejski spent on coffee in his mansion!

This is an example of excellent cash management. The single mother analysed her cash, matched her expenditure to it, and in so doing, improved the quality of the food for her children. This always appears to be a benefit, as quality always improves when you start to think in this way.

It's not rocket science, but rather the simple management of the money available to you. Unfortunately, because the minutiae of running your business tie you down, it is easy to lose sight of these basics.

This book is intended to make you think of your business as a cash generator, creating opportunities to release the cash that is already in your business, creating more wealth for you. It will show how, by using the principles of sound cash management, it is even possible to borrow money at 0% interest. Once you start looking at your business solely as a cash generator, you will prosper and be on track to make the profits you've always hoped for.

2 WHERE'S THE MONEY?

Some months ago, we ran a cash management course at a successful company that was looking for money to buy a new building. We arrived, met the management team, and started to explain to their sceptical staff the 'think cash' approach and the principles behind it.

We explained that, with our help, they were going to find the money required *from within* their company. The team looked doubtful, but to get them involved, I started off by asking what money they had in the business. After some interesting – but frankly useless – suggestions, the most junior manager said, 'Well, we do have a tankful of petrol in the yard that nobody uses. We could sell it for more than £5,000.' It broke the deadlock and helped them look at other areas of their business where there was money. By 5.00pm they had found £63,000, but by that stage they weren't sure that they wanted to spend it on a new building after all.

Experience has taught me that you can find money in every company; fair enough, it's unusual for it to come from a petrol tank in the yard, but the funds are actually flowing through the business. The 'think cash' principle releases this money so that you can use it effectively to build your company. You do this by maximising the use of every single penny running through your company.

Look at it like this:

- the money moving through your company is called your 'cash flow'
- cash comes in from sales and goes out to pay expenses (including suppliers), so some cash is constantly on the move
- a positive cash flow occurs when there is more money coming in than going out
- a negative cash flow occurs when there is more money going out than coming in

When you have a negative cash flow, you have to borrow to keep your business alive. This is not always wrong or dangerous, *but* you must have planned for it and you *must* know how long the negative cash flow situation you are borrowing to survive is going to last. To work this out, you need to know:

- when this negative cash-flow period is going to happen
- why it happened in the first place
- how long it will be before it corrects itself

For example, when a company starts up it will usually experience negative cash flow for several months. The reason is obvious: it takes time for sales revenue to reach a level where the money coming in covers that which is going out. Similarly, when you borrow to expand your business, there could easily be several months of negative cash flow before the benefits of the investment turn your cash flow positive. In all these situations it is essential that the speed at which you are burning through the money – known as the 'churn rate' – is correctly monitored.

To be honest, this should have been taken into account and calculated *before* you started your company or embarked upon any expansion, but many companies don't bother. Normally, somebody gets an idea, jots down a few figures on the back of an envelope, sees a profit, gets all excited about the opportunity that has just opened up and forges ahead without sitting down and planning it properly and working out the flow of money.

However it's happened to you, though, when your business is running with a negative cash flow you *must* turn it into a positive cash flow as soon as you possibly can. If you don't take action, you'll go under.

So let's go back to the money in your company. Where do you find it? And once you have found it, how do you release it into the business to put you on the road to positive cash flow? To begin, look at your debtors – the money owed to the company.

Debtors and creditors

Every company is owed money, so every company has debtors – even your local corner shop. In fact, there is no point in going into business unless you create them. Debtors are those customers who have bought things on credit or with a credit card. The money from credit card purchases can take three to four working days to reach your bank but some banks can improve on this, so shop around until you find one that can credit your account within two working days. The Royal Bank of Scotland, among others, offers this service, so do check with your local branch; you could gain a day. The credit card business is a very competitive one, which means that if your bank won't reduce the number of days from four, ask all the other High Street banks until you find the one that *will* clear it into your bank faster and then move your account there. This will give you the additional benefit of free banking for a year.

Another area where we can increase the cash in the business is to look at your creditors – the people to whom *you* owe money. While you're not paying your creditors, the money is still in your bank account. I understand that you probably haven't paid them because you don't have the money to do so, but when you *do* have the funds, always wait until the due date to pay them. While you are not paying them you have that money to use for the benefit of your own business.

Cost of sales, stock and expenses

The **cost of sales** (COS) is another area where you can increase the money available to you. As you've probably guessed, COS is made up of all the money that goes into creating the product or services that your company offers. Suppliers are always worried that their customers are going to go elsewhere, so make sure you review and renegotiate prices and rates regularly. The improved margins you get as a result will mean more cash for your business.

There is also money to be found in your **stock**. Try to keep on top of this, as it can creep up on you. Again, review your costs and terms with suppliers regularly, and remember that every time you succeed in getting a better price, you're putting more money into your business.

Your **expenses** are also an easy source of additional money. Each time you reduce them, you're reducing your outgoings and making even more cash available.

Assets

Assets are another source of cash and should all be seen as income generators. (See Chapters 3 and 4 for more information on the various types of asset you own.)

To calculate how good your assets are, find out how much interest would be paid on the money you'd receive if they were sold and the proceeds deposited in your bank account. The basic rule is that each of your assets must create an income that is higher than the interest that would have been earned by leaving that money in the bank. Otherwise, what is the point of spending money on an asset when you could have done just that – left it in the bank? If your assets aren't earning you any money, sell them and buy something that will give you a better return, or simply bank the money you receive for them.

Motivation

The principle of effective cash management is to use all the money in the company as much as possible: you really need it to work for you, and work hard. To do this, set yourself targets.

These are the ones you talk to yourself about when looking in the mirror every morning.

Michael Vaughan, the English cricket captain who led the Ashes-winning team in that exciting series of summer 2005, understood the importance of personal targets. When he became captain, he gave his players a poem by Dale Wimbrow (see **www.theguyin theglass.com** for more information):

When you get what you want in your struggle for
pelf *(sic)*,
And the world makes you King for a day,
Then go to the mirror and look at yourself,
And see what that guy has to say.

For it isn't your Father, or Mother, or Wife,
Who judgement upon you must pass.
The feller whose verdict counts most in your life
Is the guy staring back from the glass.

He's the feller to please, never mind all the rest,
For he's with you clear up to the end,
And you've passed your most dangerous, difficult test
If the guy in the glass is your friend.

You may be like Jack Horner and 'chisel' a plum,
And think you're a wonderful guy,
But the man in the glass says you're only a bum
If you can't look him straight in the eye.

You can fool the whole world down the pathway
   of years,
And get pats on the back as you pass,
But your final reward will be heartaches and tears
If you've cheated the guy in the glass.

Obviously this is highly relevant to successful sports
stars, but it's just as true for small business owners.
When you set yourself a target, remember that you're
setting them for the guy or girl in the glass.

So how do you go about setting these targets? You do it by
analysing your debtors, stock and creditors, and then setting
targets that allow you to monitor your progress towards
attaining your goal: increasing your company's money pool.

The X figure

The best way to set targets is to take your debtors, creditors
and stock and relate them to your sales on a weekly basis. You

do this by dividing your total sales (including VAT) by 52. For simplicity, we call this our X figure.

For example, Smith & Jones Ltd (this example is a real one, but we've changed the company name) have a turnover of £1 million. Once VAT is added, this increases to £1.175 million. The X figure is £22,596: 1,175,000 divided by 52. Using the X figure and their balance sheet:

1. We take their debtors (the money owed to them) and divide them by the X figure.
2. We then do the same with the creditors (amount they owe) and the stock.

The results are as follows:

Debtors	=	£226,000	=	10 weeks (22,596 × 10)
Creditors	=	£180,768	=	8 weeks
Stock	=	£203,364	=	9 weeks

Smith & Jones Ltd are desperate to reduce their overdraft, which is getting out of control. Their plan is to *reduce* their debtor and stock weeks (i.e. to get people to pay them quicker), whilst at the same time *increasing* their creditor weeks (i.e. paying other people more slowly – within reason). To find out how close they are to their targets, they need to record their position in each area every week. They'll then be able to see how close they are to reaching their goal of reducing the overdraft.

Their targets are:

- get debtors to pay two weeks earlier = £45,192
- pay creditors two weeks later = £45,192
- reduce the stock by two weeks = £45,192
- total cash to be created = £135,576

At the beginning of the exercise their overdraft is £80,000 and growing. After they have been working towards their targets for just a matter of weeks, the overdraft will start to shrink. As long as they keep focused on their targets, they will see the benefits to their cash flow and soon will move into the black – all before they've even looked at getting better prices from suppliers and cutting down on expenses.

It sounds simple, doesn't it? It is, as long as you remember to keep your eye on the ball. Keep the X figure in your head at all times and continue to look for new ways to meet – and then beat – those targets. Make it a habit.

Longer-term solutions to negative cash flow

Above, we looked at the short-term measures we can take to ease cash-flow problems. It's in your business's interests, though, to look for long-term solutions so that the company can get on to a more stable footing.

To get to the root of the problem, you need to know whether your current sales are high enough to cover your overheads. Obviously, if you keep having cash-flow crises, the answer is 'no'. Before you go any further, then, you must work out exactly how many sales you need each day to cover your overheads. We'll refer to this figure throughout this chapter as your **daily sales figure**.

Does this sound too simplistic? Well, it is simple, and logical, too, but you wouldn't believe the number of companies that don't know this basic fact. You'd also be surprised by how many people don't know what their daily break-even sales figure is. Very few companies actually relate their sales to a daily figure, and this is essential if they're going to survive.

It's easy to calculate the magic number if you compile a cash-flow chart, as shown in Chapter 3. Look at the 'cash out' column and work out the total amount of money going out over, say, three months. By dividing this by the number of days in the chosen period, we have the 'daily cash out figure', which, naturally, becomes the 'daily cash in figure' (because you need to bring in more than is going out). This final figure, then, is your 'daily sales figure'. This number is crucial: if your daily sales don't average this figure, you're in trouble. Once you average more than the daily sales figure on a regular basis, and then make certain that you are paid by agreed deadlines, your cash-flow problems will slowly dissolve and life will become easier.

Once you know the specific daily sales figure, the next stage is to work out what you need to do to reach it. In other words, you need to know how many calls you need to make each day to get the required number of sales.

One of the biggest sales problems for small companies is the 'hiccup' syndrome. Business tends to be a bit feast or famine. The sales team is working very hard, making and going to many appointments and, hopefully, getting lots of orders in as a result. It's at this relatively successful stage that the problem can hit, though: the team then has to spend time sorting out those orders and making certain that they are properly delivered. While they are doing this, they don't have enough time to make further appointments, with the result that their orders come through in batches and the sales graph looks as though it is 'hiccuping'.

Aiming for a daily sales figure will go some way towards curing these hiccups and making for a smoother ride. When you're working out how to reach this number, think about:

1. The number of phone calls you need to make to arrange enough sales visits.
2. The number of visits you need to get the right number of sales.
3. The amount of time taken up negotiating and finalising that order.

In analysing the figures and setting targets in this way, you break down each job required in order to achieve your daily sales figure, and identify the individual actions needed to reach your daily cash figure. This makes the whole process less woolly and much easier to manage.

Once you have set your targets, you have to make certain that your salespeople:

- are aware of them – they can't hit targets if they don't know that they exist
- understand why these figures have been set at the level they have
- realise their importance to the whole future of the company – people are much more likely to follow your lead if you explain to them why their actions are needed and what the overall impact will be
- report regularly to their line manager (if it's not you) about progress (or the lack of it)

Once you've made sure that the relevant people know they have to keep you up to speed, you should have an early warning of the next hiccough, while at the same time having greater control over your sales team. For example, if they're failing to reach the target figures on phone calls or visits – even if sales are good – this is an indication that, unless they increase the number of visits and phone appointments, at some point in the future there will be another cash-flow crisis.

Don't be distracted by a run of successes or good days: it *is* important to celebrate, but guard against complacency. Keep aiming for your targets so that you can survive the bad days when they come.

My own background is in sales and, having run many different sales forces over the years, I've learned that for them to be effective, they must have targets that are higher than those they are currently achieving. Salespeople will always moan about targets, but if they're good, they'll always aim to reach them. Your job is to make certain that you set a target that is realisable while being set just a little bit higher than the figure that your salespeople feel they can reach – while making certain that this figure is one that allows you to make a profit.

Things should be looking up now. The next step is to reduce your 'daily cash out figure'.

3
THE CASH-FLOW CHART

The best way of managing your cash when you run a small business is to make your cash-flow chart your new best friend. Remember, it's more important than your profit and loss account or balance sheet because it tells you:

- how much cash you have in the business
- how much you can spend today
- when the cash will run out unless you do something about it

If someone warned you that you were going to run out of money in three months' time, you'd have enough notice to do something about it. Without a cash-flow chart, though, you don't have any type of early warning system and you could turn up to the office one day only to find yourself unable even to write a cheque.

Drawing up the chart

I suggest a 'back to basics' approach to this. Go to your local stationer's and buy an accounting pad with three columns and a box of pencils with rubbers at the end. (Notice that I'm not using a computer. Why? Because I've found that by writing everything down on paper first, I get a 'feel' for exactly how the money flow is running. I'm sure that eventually you will put it into an Excel spreadsheet, but let's start with pencil and paper.)

Fill in the columns as shown in the example on pp. 24–26. To start with, write MONTH 1 (or the actual name of the month, if you prefer) at the top on the left. In the second column, add the heading CASH OUT. Beneath that, put the total of all the standing orders and direct debits going out this month. Then, as in the example, add in things like salaries and so on to give you a subtotal.

Underneath this, list all your other creditors under three headings:

1. Those you must pay.
2. Those you would like to pay.
3. Those you can delay paying if pushed.

Put a subtotal next to each heading in the adjacent column and include a grand total at the bottom.

You now have all your company's outgoings for the month split into subheadings:

- direct debits that will go out automatically whatever you do, provided you have adequate funds
- bills that have to be paid
- people you would like to pay
- people you can delay paying if you have to

Now, head the third column CASH IN and beneath this heading note down any money due in from debtors this month as well as money currently in the bank. Do not include a figure that you *think* might come in – work it out properly. (You did this earlier when you were calculating your debtor days.) If your debtor days are 30 then your CASH IN will be last month's sales, and if they are 60, then your CASH IN will be your sales from two months ago.

When you're putting this information together, remember that while your sales are rising, you will get in more each month than your chart shows; if they start to fall, you will be getting in *less* each month. The chart will reflect this too, giving you time to take some preventative action, whether it be getting out there and selling your products yourself, or getting your sales team (if you have one) to move up a gear.

Once you have done this, total up the CASH IN side.

....

The difference between the two columns tells you whether there will be enough money for the month ahead. Repeat this process for the next few months. As you already know how much money will come in next month, and as most suppliers give 30 days' credit, you know what you will be paying out next month. This way your chart will be accurate, allowing you to predict the future with a reasonable degree of confidence. Your aim is to be cash-positive three months ahead.

MONTH 1	**Cash Out**	**Cash In**
Money due in from debtors		
Money in bank account		
Total cash available		
Money due out		
Monthly standing orders (incl loans)		
Salaries		
PAYE/NI		
Office expenses		
Telephone		
Utilities		
Rent/Rates		
Miscellaneous		
Petty cash		
VAT		
Subtotal		

Creditors:

Must pay

Like to pay

Can delay

Total Creditors

TOTAL OUT

Difference carried forward

MONTH 2

Money due in from debtors

In bank

Total cash available

Money due out

Monthly standing orders
   (incl loans)

Salaries

PAYE/NI

Office expenses

Telephone

Utilities

Rent/Rates

Miscellaneous

Petty cash

VAT

Subtotal

MONTH 2 – *continued*	**Cash Out**	**Cash In**
Creditors:		
Must pay		
Like to pay		
Can delay		
Total creditors		
TOTAL OUT		
Difference carried forward		

Reducing risk the Branson way

Richard Branson, of Virgin fame, has an unbreakable rule, which is to 'limit the downside'. He only takes bold steps if he knows that he can limit the risk. An example of this was the way he set up his airline, Virgin Atlantic. From his cash-flow sheets, he knew that the income generated by the music side of his business would allow him to cover the costs of leasing a Boeing jet if he could get the jet at the right price. Even if he didn't sell enough seats, the cash-flow projections told him that he could survive for the first few years. Although it looked to the rest of the world as though he was betting his shirt on the project, he knew he wasn't. Without an efficient cash-flow chart, though, he could never have stuck to his rule of limiting the downside.

Using the chart

Now back to reality. So you've drawn up your cash-flow chart and gained some information about what the financial future may hold. Your next step is to start using that information.

Begin by asking yourself whether you have enough money coming in to pay the direct debits this month. Once you know this, you can lay out a schedule of payments relating to when the rest of the money comes in, so that when each £500 comes in you know the exact bill that money will pay. It is easy for accountants to produce cash-flow charts but their charts are based on longer periods, normally months. The one you are producing must – and will – relate to the fact that money doesn't come in regularly each day, but rather that it comes in 'lumps' and those lumps don't necessarily come in when you need them, or even when you predict that they will.

Once you have worked out who you need to pay and when, look at the 'cash in' side of your chart to see whether you can afford it. If there is not enough on this side to pay everything, don't panic. Your cash-flow chart has allowed you to see the future, which makes it easier for you to start planning. You can now move on to the next stage, which is to look at ways that some of your debtors can be persuaded to pay a little earlier. Even if there is enough money coming in, it's better still to get it in even sooner. Turn to Chapter 6 for more information on this.

4 MAXIMISING YOUR ASSETS

To make the best use of your cash, you need to get the most out of all your company's assets, which we looked at briefly in Chapter 2. In short, assets are the resources a company owns that can generate profit.

Normally, assets are split up into the following categories:

- current assets
- fixed assets
- intangible assets
- liquid assets

So far, we have concentrated on **current** assets, such as debtors, stock and the cash in the bank. **Fixed** assets are items such as land, machinery and buildings. They are things you can see – and even kick if you need to. **Intangible** assets, on the other hand, include goodwill, patents and any copyrights your business holds. They have a value, but it is undefined, so it's difficult to attribute a price to them: in a sense, they're only worth what someone will pay for them on a given day. If they're listed on a balance sheet at all, it tends to be as a nominal figure. Your **liquid** assets are either those funds that are kept in the form of cash, or anything you hold that can be quickly turned into cash, such as fast-moving stock.

A simple way to improve your cash position is to look at these fixed, intangible and liquid assets to make certain that they are giving you an adequate return. There is a simple yardstick you can use in order to determine this: ask yourself whether these assets are making you more money than they would if they were turned into cash and left in the bank. If they are earning their keep for you, fine. If not, do something about it – quickly. For example, let's look at your fixed assets, such as the building you're working in. Is it leasehold or free-hold? If it's leasehold, how long is the lease? Does what is left of the lease have any value? If so, would you benefit from realising that value and moving to different, cheaper pre-mises? If your property is freehold, how long is there left on the mortgage, or is it totally unencumbered? Could you release the money tied up in your property to put more cash into the business?

Leasing

If you own your premises, most accountants will tell you that the easiest way to put money into your business is to do a

sale and leaseback. Under this arrangement, you sell your building to a property company, who then immediately give you a long-term lease on the building, usually with three- or five-year rent reviews. It is a simple transaction. You don't have to move from your premises and the money from the sale will be in your bank account within a matter of weeks. This is something you can do even if you haven't paid off the mortgage you took out to buy the building, as the value will inevitably have risen, and the increase in value can go straight back into your business.

Sounds fantastic, doesn't it? Yes, but the reality is often less so. In my opinion, it's much better simply to remortgage the building. You end up with the same amount of money, and it is just as easy. In fact, it is even easier than a sale and leaseback, as you don't have to agree a new lease. Also, when you remortgage, you still own the property and will therefore be able to benefit from any future increase in property prices. With a sale and leaseback, you give your new landlord those benefits. You also have to pay rent, which will keep going up; all commercial leases have a clause that allows rents only to rise, not fall. With a mortgage, the repayments will be roughly the same, *but* they could go down should the interest rate fall.

While sale and leaseback leaves me cold when it comes to property, leasing *can* be an important and useful tool in other areas. It allows you to put your money into the income-generating side of your business, rather than tying it up in such items as cars and furniture, which eventually lose their value. Car leases are a perfect example of this for a small business. Many businesses accept that, in the interests of their own efficiency and vehicle reliability, their cars need to be upgraded regularly, and most are replaced every three years, which is the usual length of a hire purchase (HP) agreement. Once the HP is finished, the car is traded in and used as the deposit for a new one. If you *lease* a car rather than buy it, you can then sell all your vehicles and inject the proceeds from the sale into the business. Your lease payments then take the place of the HP payments. Even though there's little difference in the payment terms, the big benefit is that they don't show up as borrowings on your company's balance sheet, which will help if you need to go to the bank to raise more money. Also, in leasing your vehicles, you benefit both from the injection into your business of the cash lump sum received from the sale of the HP cars, and from being able to upgrade your company's vehicles regularly once the period of the lease has elapsed.

There is a further advantage of leasing: you can include servicing in the lease agreement. Your monthly vehicle costs are then fixed, so you don't get a surprise repair bill when you can least afford it. Like most things, cars always break down at the worst possible time – normally when you have a cash-flow crisis. By leasing a car and making sure that servicing and replacement cars are included in the terms of the lease, you have one less potential financial headache to worry about.

You can also lease machinery. To remain competitive, you ought to replace your machinery on a regular basis to ensure that it remains efficient and in good condition. Also, depending on the industry you're in, you may need to keep up with changes in technology, and you'll need to budget appropriately for such updates. However, if a cash problem hits the company, leaving you desperate for extra funds, you may raid the money set aside for machine replacement. You'll be out of the crisis, certainly, but you'll then have to start all over again saving to replace that piece of equipment. If this keeps happening, you'll still have the same equipment in 30 years' time. How many small engineering companies are there around the country with 30-year-old equipment? Hundreds! On the other hand, if they were to lease the equipment, they wouldn't have to pay out large sums of capital, but rather a monthly figure that becomes part of their monthly overhead cost. At the end of the lease period that piece of equipment is taken away and immediately replaced with the latest model. The company's equipment is now always up to date, which means that the quality of their work should be that much better and their pricing that much more competitive.

Therefore, if you have been putting funds aside to replace your equipment, put this money into the business and lease the new machines you require today. If you don't have a fund and are about to borrow on an HP agreement, again lease the machinery, because then the payments become a business expense, which will benefit your cash flow. There may also be a benefit to your tax position, but this is best discussed with your accountant.

Don't stop at the cars and machinery, though. If your offices are visited regularly by your customers, think about selling *all* the office fittings – yes, the desks, the chairs, the filing cabinets and even the photocopier – and leasing new ones. The money you receive from the sale is then released into your business. A significant additional benefit is that the image you present to your customers will improve, as they will feel that they are dealing with a highly successful, growing business. Don't get too carried away, though. It's important that you don't end up in an 'emperor's new clothes' situation: what you do is still more important than how your reception area looks. There are also some assets that you *shouldn't* lease, such as computers. As IT equipment develops so quickly and there is always a fixed period on the lease, you may not be able to upgrade your equipment quickly enough to keep up with improved software or hardware. Similarly, never take out a fixed lease on equipment that you'll only need for a short time, for exactly the same reason – you'll have to stay with it for the period of the lease and let it gather dust.

Intangible assets

Finally, look at your intangible assets. Don't neglect them. For example, everyone has heard of Intel, which makes the computer chips that we find in most of our computers. What do you think is worth most to the company: the machines, their Pentium chips or the rights to the intellectual property that created them?

The answer is the intellectual property rights – their intangible assets. In fact, for many of the world's most successful companies the patents, copyrights, brands and other intangible assets are worth far more than such physical assets as factories, offices and stock. Intangible assets often count for little in accounting terms, but intellectual property rights in the sole ownership of the company can be very valuable. As we've seen, Intel would be nothing without those designs for its chips.

Use Intel as your inspiration when you look at your company. Examine everything, from the plans to the designs, the ideas and even the data you hold. You could surprise yourself and discover that something you've taken for granted for many years is actually of enormous value.

Dell Computers is another example of intangible

assets being used wisely. The company has an advanced logistical supply chain along with a superb ability to get people to its website so that they place orders. The American stock market looks on both of these as an intangible asset that the company has created through developing its very own area of excellence of its own making. As mentioned above, these assets don't appear on the balance sheet – because you can't really 'value' them per se – but their notional value to the stock market has meant that Dell's share price is higher than that of other PC manufacturers who don't have such sophisticated systems.

Microsoft is another company where the knowledge generated has become an intangible asset that has increased their value many times over. The same goes for Google. When Google was launched on the US stock market, it was valued at more than 100 times its earnings, due to the value of its search engine, which again is not a recordable asset and therefore isn't in its balance sheet. Few of us have Google's millions at our disposal, but you should still find out whether it's possible to sell any of your intangible assets. You could even set up a licensing deal whereby another company can take your product and sell it. There is lots of potential here, so don't dismiss your intangible assets. If they can be turned into cash, you'll find useful extra money for your company that can come into the business without any cost of sale.

Tracking your assets

Managing your assets is essential if you're going to rein in your cash flow. Assets show up on your balance sheet. Many people panic when faced with balance sheets and similar financial paperwork, mainly because they don't understand them. In this section, we'll look at the basic principles of your accounts so that you can see how everything fits together.

The balance sheet

A balance sheet is a snapshot of a company *on a given day*. That doesn't sound like much, but looking at one carefully can tell you a lot about the financial health of a business.

In broad strokes, a balance sheet is a list of a company's assets and liabilities: items that you owe and debts you have, or money that is owed to you. They have to balance (hence the name) with the capital employed in the business, plus the profits or losses that the company has made *on a particular day*. This point is a crucial one, as this is where a balance sheet differs from a profit and loss account, which tells you what happened over a period of time.

Assets appear on one side of a balance sheet, liabilities on the other. Beneath the 'assets' heading, list all items that generate income, such as:

- **stock** – items you can sell and generate income from
- **debtors** – money owed to the company
- **money in the bank** – which generates income by earning interest
- **profits** – all the profits and losses of the company added together
- **fixed assets** – buildings, vehicles, equipment, etc, which can be sold if necessary
- **prepayments** – bills you have paid in advance, such as utility bills or insurance, are assets, even though they don't generate income in their own right
- **intellectual property rights**
- **petty cash**

On the other side, to balance it up, list items that *cost* you money:

- **creditors**
- **VAT, if appropriate, and any other costs relating to Her Majesty's Revenue and Customs**

(HMRC; which now manages all issues formerly controlled by the Inland Revenue)

- bank overdraft
- credit-card balances
- loans
- **accruals** – bills that you know that you will have to pay

Add up the totals in each list, and then subtract the liabilities from the assets. This will give you a plus or minus figure, usually described as the net assets (if a positive number) or net liabilities (if negative).

Next, start another list. This is to work out the money required by the business so that it can function, and is known as the **capital employed**. It's made up of:

- **share capital** – the money put into the company to start it up in the first place
- **long-term loans** – any loans taken out to build the business
- **the previous year's profit or loss**

The total of this list must balance with the first calculation. The figure that makes it balance is the profit/loss figure, which is the total amount of profit or loss made by the company since it was formed.

We are only really interested in the debtors, stock and creditors figures, all three of which relate to the last 12 months' turnover to create our X figure, as explained in Chapter 2.

Let's return to the example in Chapter 2, where we saw the effect of reducing both debtors and stock by £8,000 while increasing creditors by £8,000. Once this has been successful you would expect the £24,000 created to go into in the bank on the asset side, as we have increased the money available within the company by £24,000. This is what you would expect to happen, and it does – but only briefly. In reality, this money will be used to clear debt elsewhere in the business, or to buy further assets.

To manage your cash in the best possible way, keep looking at the balance sheet and then concentrate all your efforts on reducing debtors and stock while increasing the creditors. Make sure you know when your cash is going to come in and go out. The best way to trace your money flow is via a cash-flow chart. Before we look at how to do that, though, we need to look at the profit and loss account.

The profit and loss account

The profit and loss account – commonly abbreviated and referred to as 'P & L' – is a record of transactions over a given period.

To explain how a P & L works, let's buy some bricks. We'll buy them for £10,000 and sell for £20,000, giving a profit of

£10,000. This profit is the **gross profit**, as it doesn't take into account any expenses incurred by buying the bricks. The sum left once those figures have been taken into account is the **net profit**.

In this example, the expenses incurred would be the cost of storing and delivering those bricks. If those costs come to £5,000, our net profit would be £5,000.

Written as a P & L account, this transaction would look like this:

Sales	£20,000	
Buying cost	(£10,000)	
Gross profit		£10,000
Expenses		(£5,000)
Net profit		£5,000

It looks simple, but there are some issues to consider. On the balance sheet there is no disputing your debtor and creditor figures, so you can safely work out your X figure without fooling yourself. It's not quite the same on the P & L, though, because the expenses can have different values.

To illustrate using the example above, your expenses could have been made up of different costs, such as carriage. This could have been a one-off delivery of bricks, rather than a regular part of your business. For a one-off expense, you'd have to hire a lorry to deliver the bricks. On the other hand, if the deal *was* part of your regular business, you may already have the lorry. You could then spread the cost over several journeys and could possibly reduce the total expenses from, say, £5,000 to £4,000, which would increase the profit from £5,000 to £6,000.

On the other hand, even if you owned the lorry, you might decide that it would only be correct to include it in your figures at the price it costs to hire it, in which case your profits would come back down to £5,000.

If you do this transaction routinely as part of your business, and you supply bricks all over the country every day, then the office, staff and all those other expenditures of the company are included. If you're at all unsure about these issues, check with your accountant or contact HMRC for advice: visit them online at **www.hmrc.gov.uk.**

The potential for confusion here can lead companies on to dangerous ground. In Chapter 1, we looked at how in Next in the 1980s showed a profit of £100 million while having a cash shortfall of £250 million. Because of those high profits, its shares rose and everyone felt that it was a company to follow, while in fact it was running out of money.

At the time, I wondered how that could happen, but recently I have been helping a company in similar circumstances. On a £1 million turnover they were showing a £150,000 profit, but had no money because they were owed over £300,000. When we looked at those debts we soon realised that over £120,000 would never be collected and at some point this sum would have to be written off. The problem was that the company wasn't in a position to do that without incurring the wrath of the bank. The company was surviving on an overdraft and the bank was happy to support them because of those profits they were seeing on the P & L account.

So, the P & L tells you how successful your business is over a given period of time. It's a very useful barometer, because if you're not making any profit, you'll run out of money very quickly. Keeping a close eye on your P & L means that you'll be able to spot potential danger signs and address the issues promptly before things get out of hand.

In addition to being a useful tool in keeping the bank manager on side, a P & L also affects how much tax you have to pay, as it is those profits showing on the P & L that decide the amount of corporation tax you will be liable for.

5 THE BUSINESS PLAN

If your business is ready to grow, the best way to make sure that it does so within appropriate commercial restraints is to write a business plan.

The best type of business plan is a short one; ideally, it should be no more than four pages long. For our purposes here, it's fine to keep it short, because you're writing it only for yourself and your partners. Formulating your thoughts in this way, before you go ahead with the next stage in the development of your business, will mean that you and your partners know:

- what you're going to do
- how long it will take
- whether it's likely to work

You can, of course, expand the plan at a later date if you need to use it for a different purpose, such as to raise money, but at this stage, keep it simple and keep it focused on you.

Remember that business plans don't have to be confined just to the start-up phases of a new company. It's a good idea to prepare one before you launch any project, so that you're thinking in advance of the three key points above. Be prepared to modify the plan as the project progresses.

Putting the business plan down on paper helps you to clarify your ideas about the course of action you're planning to take. Because you're looking at the project in detail, you'll find that new ideas and approaches occur to you as you work through each section. Also, you'll start to see potential problems that may not have struck you before, which is no bad thing: identifying problems is the first step towards coming up with an effective solution to them. It may even become startlingly apparent that the project just won't work. Yes, you may be disappointed, but it's better to find out now – before you've spent even more time and hard-earned cash on it – than discover its limitations years down the line.

Eventually you will end up with a very clear plan of next steps. This will give you the confidence to move forward, safe in the knowledge that you have looked at your business plan from all angles and know exactly how much money you need. As a bonus, if you need to raise money for the project, the plan will already be clear in your mind and this will make it much easier to convince potential backers.

Once you have completed your business plan, you'll be able to use it as a useful tool in many different ways, such as when during negotiations with suppliers. It gives a professional veneer to your business when you're talking to others, showing not only that you have taken the time to understand the market, but that you know what is happening in and to that market, and how your company is going to succeed in it. Your supplier will feel much more confident about working with you: if you know the market so well, you're much more likely to sell their products successfully to that market.

So what should a business plan include and how is it made up? There are two main parts: the figures and the words.

The figures

Before you start writing the plan, work out a simple cash-flow chart so that you can see that it is possible to make money from this venture, and calculate exactly how much cash you will need to fund it.

In broad strokes:

1. Round up (or down) all figures to the nearest hundred or thousand.
2. Make simple assumptions, such as that all bills will be paid at the end of the month following the

invoice. (This is what I call 'bucket accounting' and it tells you very quickly whether it will work financially or not.)

3. So that you are not caught out later, it's wise to *double* the expenses you think you may incur and *halve* the sales you think you will make. This gives you a 'worst-case scenario'.

I normally work out my initial cash-flow charts for 12 months, as I have found that projections any further into the future start to lose touch with reality. Because you're excited about the project, you forget that it may fail and so assume that the projected growth will continue at the same rate year on year. On paper, it looks so simple and, yes, it *could* happen like that, but it's not likely to. You can accurately predict the first six months but beyond that you're in the realm of guesswork. It's very tempting to get carried away and produce wilder and wilder figures that *appear* to show that by the time you reach years four and five, you'll be a multi-millionaire. If you restrict your plans to 12 or 18 months hence, however, you're much more likely to keep your feet on the ground.

This approach can create a problem when you pitch to a bank or investor, as they always ask for at least three years' projections – sometime five years'. In such cases, you have no choice other than to give them the projections – but make clear that they are just that.

The words

If the bucket cash-flow projection works, then prepare it as an addendum and move on to the wording of your business plan. My basic business plan is simple and has the following headings:

1. **Introduction.** Here, you simply introduce your idea, and the reasons behind it. For example, are you expanding your range of services because customers have been repeatedly asking for something you don't currently offer? Or has technology moved on, meaning that you can upgrade an existing product?

2. **The product or service itself.** In other words, the nuts and bolts of exactly what it is. Is it a new type of car wax that doesn't streak, for example? An environmentally friendly oven cleaner?

3. **Current financial position.** A brief summary of the financial health of your business.

4. **The funding requirement.** A brief explanation of how much money you need, broken down into how it will be spent (for example, £X on marketing, £Y on research and development, and so on).

5. **Management and personnel.** A brief description of who is going to do what if the project goes forward.

6. **Market.** Who is your product aimed at?

7. **Competition.** Even if your product or service is unique, there's still 'competition' for it in that people are currently spending their money somewhere else on something else. How can your offering grab their attention?

8. **Route to market.** How are you going to sell the product?

9. **Market potential.** How many customers could you feasibly reach?

10. **Financial projections.** Cash-flow projections and a simple profit and loss account, so you know at what point the project will move into profit.

11. **Debtor and creditor sensitivity analysis.** Write down how sensitive the plan is to delays in debtors paying you, or to your creditors demanding faster payment.

12. **SWOT Analysis.** List Strengths and Weaknesses of the project as well as Opportunities for, and Threats to it, and the business.

13. **Conclusion.**

As this draft of the business plan is purely for use *inside* your company, keep it brief and aim to write no more than 50 words on each section. The whole aim of producing this version of the plan is so that you can collate your thoughts, and by keeping the word count on each section so low, you're forced to think hard about the absolutely vital points you want to mention. You can flag up potential problems too – and suggest solutions to them – as you go along.

The sensitivity analysis of your debtors and creditors is an essential part of your planning process, as it is an aid to working out the risks.

The SWOT analysis is a great help in clarifying in your own mind the risks you are likely to encounter. It is also very useful if you go to the next level and need to convince an external partner or backer of the validity of your idea. You have all the relevant information to hand. As mentioned above, SWOT stands for:

- **S**trengths
- **W**eaknesses
- **O**pportunities
- **T**hreats

It's easy to identify strengths and opportunities, but listing weaknesses and threats is more difficult. You wouldn't be doing this if you didn't see the opportunities, but discipline yourself to find the same number of weaknesses and threats as strengths and opportunities. Many of them will be potential problems rather than real ones, but it's still useful to think through these issues – and act on them if you need to.

Bankers and venture capitalists *love* SWOT and sensitivity analyses, by the way, so this is another useful section to complete in case you ever need to turn the business plan into a more formal document.

One of the major reasons for new companies failing is people not looking deeply enough into their business idea before committing themselves to starting the company. Then, when the business is up and running, they run into unanticipated problems.

Identifying problems in advance – and finding solutions to them – is a tremendous advantage from which you will benefit before you start, and again when trying to convince others of the benefits of your idea. They will be reassured by your having clearly thought deeply about the issues your business may face.

The popular television programme *Dragon's Den* features people pitching their business ideas to five successful entrepreneurs. As you watch, it becomes obvious that very few of the contestants have actually fully worked out all the future pitfalls of their idea. Few appear to have written a business plan, and those who have appear to have written it while wearing rose-tinted spectacles, in the hope that they will convince the dragons of the merits of their brilliant idea. Learn from these poor candidates' mistakes, then, and realise that your killer idea has to be well thought out before anyone will give it any money.

In summary, then, a business plan will help you:

- identify and research your target market
- work out how to reach customers
- identify areas of risk
- find solutions to potential problems
- work out how much funding you need

Don't leave it in your desk drawer

Once you have written your business plan, don't leave it to moulder in a dusty corner of the office. Like your cash-flow chart, see your business plan as a 'living' document. Whether things are going well or badly, use it and update it regularly.

As your business develops and changes, so will your opportunities. To keep the company aligned with this progress, the business plan needs to change as well. If you keep updating your plan, when another opportunity turns up you can work out whether to include it and make even more money! Alternatively, should a problem appear and you need to borrow to overcome it, you'll already have a document ready to use, which makes it easier to prepare for the inevitable bank interview.

A business plan, along with your cash-flow chart, is one of the most useful tools when talking to bank managers, as they both show that you've spent time thinking about the business to which you are asking them to lend money. But remember: it doesn't matter how brilliant this business plan is on its own: the bank manager won't lend you money unless you have enough security. Turn to Chapter 18 for more information on this.

6
GETTING PAID MORE QUICKLY

If your business is in cash-flow hell, speeding up how quickly you are paid by others – often referred to as 'reducing debtor days' – can make a massive difference. This chapter looks at some of the useful techniques you can use to inject some much-needed money into the business.

Being paid quickly is an essential part of good cash management. Remember to:

1. Raise your invoices promptly

The sooner you raise the invoice, the sooner the cash will come in. Put in place a system that allows you to raise invoices immediately or as soon as is practical. Don't leave it until the end of the month or even the end of the week; sort this out *today*. If you don't look after this part of your business personally, make sure the person who manages it is on the ball.

2. Create incentives for faster payment

We looked at this issue briefly in Chapter 2. If your margins allow, offer a discount for prompt payers. All you need to do is add a short message to your invoice along the lines of:

> 'If this invoice is paid by 30 November, a discount of £25.00 may be taken.'

Make sure you don't do this too often, though, or suppliers will automatically expect it.

Some people are put off this option because of VAT issues. How can you calculate it in this situation? Our local VAT office has accepted that we can work the VAT out on the assumption that the discount is taken, but if you are at all unsure, check with your local office to make sure they are happy *before* you proceed.

3. Investigate factoring

Factoring isn't an appropriate solution for every business, but it can mean that someone else manages your debts, leaving you free to run your company. In brief, it works as follows:

- every time you raise an invoice, you transfer that debt to the factoring company
- the factoring company then immediately pays you a percentage of the invoice, which can range from 65% to 80%, depending on your deal with them

■ the factoring company then chases the debt, and when the full debt is paid, they pay you the balance of the invoice, less their charges

Therefore, you get paid up to 80% of your invoices within days of raising them.

In theory, it's a very useful tool to fund a growing company, *provided* that you have large enough margins and the factoring company chases the debts promptly. There is a problem, though. A factoring company charges you interest for the period of time between paying you and receiving payment from your customer. This means that they make more money (out of you) from late-paying customers than they do from prompt payers. As this is the only way for a factoring company to make money, it means that they have no incentive to get your money in quickly, with the result that they don't tend to start chasing your debts until they are at least 30 days old. Two of our suppliers factor their debts, and four months later – even though they had sent us statements – they still hadn't asked for the money. This is great for us, but a disaster for them.

Obviously, to protect themselves, factoring companies can't allow debts to remain outstanding indefinitely: accounts have to be settled in the end or, again, they won't make any money. To guard against this, factoring companies include clauses in their contracts that allow them to return an invoice to you if your client hasn't paid within an agreed number of months (usually three, or 90 days). This means that most knowledgeable companies make a habit of only paying the factoring company about a week before the 90 days is up.

Two of my businesses have used factoring companies, with differing degrees of success. My office equipment company needed cash urgently, but the factoring company only chased after two months. This resulted in relatively high interest charges, which didn't help the company in the longer term. On the second occasion, which was with a start-up company, it worked much better: we retained control of our debt chasing so that eventually our cash management allowed us to do without them. In this case, factoring was a good option. It allowed us to build up a company when we didn't have enough money to fund its growth, by using our outstanding debtors. As soon as the company reached a reasonable size and the cash flow was healthy enough, there was no need for the factor, which had then become an added cost that we didn't need. We took the debts back and the company continued to grow from its own cash flow.

The main reason most companies use factoring is that they need a cash injection. When you engage a factoring company, it buys your current debtor list. For example, if your debtors are £150,000, the factor usually pays your company 70% of those debtors immediately – as much as £105,000. On the face of it, then, factoring looks like a great solution to cash-flow headaches. Do take great care when considering it, however: its success depends very much on your margins and the payment period too. You will only get between 70% and 80% of your invoices paid immediately; the rest comes when the customer pays. If your debtor defaults, you have to repay that 70% to 80% with interest. Also remember that even though you could receive a large cash injection from selling your debtor list, it's definitely a one-off.

4. Do something dizzy

Do something different – write a tongue-in-cheek poem, or maybe draw a cartoon – that makes your invoices stand out from the crowd. I'm not suggesting that this should be your default method for chasing up late payment, but it can work effectively if you use it wisely.

To illustrate, below is a poem we sent to Karren Brady, managing director of Birmingham City Football Club. We had acted as a supplier to them for some time and the club had paid us regularly within 14 days as per our agreement. Suddenly, payment dates started to slip. We wanted to do something to get their attention without upsetting them, so we sent them the following:

> I can't believe we're still not paid,
> We did the work and made the grade.

We moved a job to get it done
So for delay you would have none.

We're great supporters of your Club,
And want to help sell seats and grub.

Advance payment is our natural terms
But for your ease we were less firm.

Up to now you've been quite good
And paid up as you know you should.

This time it seems it's all gone wrong,
Thirty-five days late, still going strong.

We've rung and often got voicemail,
This cash delay makes us quite pale.

We can't think why it should be late
You get your money on the gate!

So please get our cheque on its way.
We'll pick it up to save delay.

We don't like being in the dark,
And our bank account is rather stark!

So take this in the way it's meant,
And get our cheque signed now and sent.

                                            Thank you

It won't win the Forward Prize for poetry, but it worked. We sent it as a fax and found out later that it had made the rounds of all the offices in the club. We very quickly got a phone call apologising for the delay and, as we're based nearby, we were able to pop over and collect the cheque. The real benefit was that we got our money without offending our customer: we still got work from the club subsequently, and were always paid on the due date.

5. Credit cards

Whatever your business, make sure you accept payment by credit card. It's a great way of injecting cash into your business quickly. We always make a point of telling customers that they can pay us in this way, and many do. It's convenient for them and wonderful for us because the amount is then in our cash flow, and our bank account benefits. Ask your bank about setting up a credit-card facility: there will be a charge, but it's well worth the investment. Remember that you get the money in your bank account within four working days: if you invoice customers on standard credit terms, you have to wait 30 days.

7
THE ORDER IS ONLY COMPLETE WHEN IT'S BEEN PAID FOR

'The cheque's in the post!' Famously, this is one of the most quoted lines in business, and do we believe it? No. Can we do anything about it? That's another problem in itself.

If you're new to business or trying to expand your customer base, you may worry that pressurising people about late payments may backfire – they may take their business elsewhere, for example. In the end, you may even convince yourself that the fault really does lie with the Royal Mail and that waiting a few more days won't really cause too many problems.

Don't go there! Why should you let late payers get away with it? The most important thing to remember about any order is that it's not completed until it's been fully paid for.

Bear this in mind at all times and don't lose any sleep whatsoever about chasing customers who owe you money. They're late, and that's the end of it. If your customer hasn't paid, the order hasn't been completed and therefore you don't want to do any more business with the company or person in question until they pay up. Your company doesn't exist to give its products or services away.

What does it matter if aggressive customers threaten you with taking away any future business? What good *is* their business if they don't pay? And remember, important as the cash is, the time they take to pay you is crucial too. Frankly, if they don't pay you promptly, you're better off without them. If they don't pay on time, you have to borrow to cover the cash-flow gap this creates, all of which is expensive. Every customer who delays payment, therefore, makes your cash position worse, reduces your profit and costs you money.

This problem becomes more apparent with new businesses, many of which seem to get their first orders from the bad payers. This is no coincidence: bad payers can spot new kids on the block before they've set foot in their office. They know that fledgling businesses want and need customers enough to let bad payers stretch out payment. These companies are past masters at waving the prospects of big orders in the future in front of new businesses. Don't fall into this trap and do take time to check out potential customers – there's more information on this in Chapter 11.

Don't panic

Let's return to the cash-flow chart and assume that it shows that there won't be enough money to cover this month's expenditure. Whatever you do, don't panic. Everyone has a short-term cash-flow problem at one time or another. The key thing here is to act quickly to sort it out, one step at a time. Don't put it off and think the problem will solve itself.

Start by focusing on your debtors, those people who owe you money. Look through the list and ring those you think can pay you if you give them a small discount. When you call them, nine times out of ten they'll come out with the classic 'it's in the post'. Don't give them the benefit of the doubt this time. Instead, make this tired old chestnut work to your advantage for once. Reply by saying, 'That's great. Actually, I was going to offer you a discount if you paid by Friday, but now that the cheque's on its way I won't need to.'

You will be surprised by how often your errant customer will castigate the Royal Mail's service, decide that the original cheque is lost, and offer to write you a new one there and then for the discounted amount. You know full well that the 'original' cheque never existed, but you will get some payment the next day. If you've been careful about the discount you offer, you won't be too far off the amount you asked for anyway. If you do use this tactic, it's essential that you make a note to start chasing this customer *early* next time, because if not, they will most likely delay payment until you offer them another discount.

This works if you have a short-term cash problem as it will put cash in the bank, quickly. When you're in financial trouble, this is your first priority, but you should *only* do this when you have a cash shortfall that you need to cover urgently. Don't use this tactic regularly, because your customers will start to expect it – which means that they get a permanent discount. Read on for further tips on prompt payment.

If you have a cash-flow problem, you can't pay your creditors. You need to find a way to delay the payment without making them take drastic action against you.

Every creditor is a debtor too

Has anyone ever telephoned you before an invoice's due date and said, 'Look, I thought I'd let you know that we have a slight cash problem and your cheque will be coming out a week later than usual?'

Probably not very often – if ever. If they did, you would probably have thanked them for letting you know and hung up, slightly dazed. Most people's reactions would be the same. It's natural when you are short of money to want to keep quiet about it; on the other hand, if you're owed money you want to know as soon as possible if your debtors have a problem.

Your next job, then, is to put this advice into practice and to ring your creditors to explain your plight and to reassure them that they'll be paid within X weeks. You will be amazed by how helpful people will be because you have told them that you have a problem and are trying to address it.

The overall result is that you'll have put two weeks' outgoings into your bank account. This means you have some cash available to meet the expenses that can't be delayed. We will cover this in more detail later, but do remember to keep your creditors on side.

These tactics will only help you out in the short term, however. You can't keep ringing up your debtors and offering them discounts to make them pay; neither can you make a habit of phoning your creditors to tell them you have a problem. They'll soon start worrying and take a firmer line with you, for which you can hardly blame them. In Chapter 8, we'll look at best practices in credit management and look at ways to get your debtors figure down, slowly but surely.

8

THE RULES OF CREDIT MANAGEMENT

In most companies, the accounts team deal with invoices for payment. Everyone hassles them for different reasons, which makes for a stressful life: the boss wants her figures; the sales reps need them to chase customers for payment; those customers in turn get shirty when they're chased. The list is endless.

To help yourself and your business, try to break this cycle. Make a friend of your contact in the accounts department and have reasonable conversations rather than slanging matches. Send some chocolates or a few bottles of wine at Christmas. The result? Your contact will help you by processing and having your invoice signed quickly. Once you have built a relationship with your contact in accounts, your debt-chasing becomes much easier, and if you then follow these simple rules of credit management, your debtor days will come down.

1. Before you supply goods, make sure the customer has agreed to your terms in writing

This is so simple and so often overlooked. There are many potential crossed wires when a deal is done. The rep thinks he agreed payment within 30 days, but the customer thinks that it's due 30 days from the end of the month following delivery.

Nothing much is done about this until after the goods have been delivered and someone is chasing payment. If the deal had been confirmed by e-mail, letter or fax, though, and the terms spelled out clearly, the issue would have been cleared up at a much earlier stage.

2. If you supply goods, make sure you get a signed delivery note

On a similar theme, if you supply physical goods to a customer, get a signature on delivery, confirming that the goods have been received in a satisfactory condition. This means that the customer cannot say that the goods were damaged during delivery as an excuse not to pay.

3. Raise the invoice and send it as soon as you can after delivery of goods. Ideally, ship them both at the same time

Until an invoice is raised, your customers can't do anything with it! The payment process will only start once your invoice has been raised and received by your customers. If you invoice promptly, you'll get paid sooner: it's as simple as that.

Ideally, you should raise the invoice before delivery. When you think about it, there are actually many businesses you pay before delivery: mail order is a good example. When I buy books online, I pay with my credit card in advance. When I book my holiday, I pay the travel company before I go. It's an accepted practice for some companies, then, so could you make it so for yours?

On the other hand, while there are many trades where people pay in advance, there are also many where they raise invoices monthly. Never fall into this trap. If you can't invoice in advance, invoice as the goods are going out of the door. If your current system means that you invoice on a monthly basis, change it today.

4. Seven days after the invoice has been dispatched, ring your customer to make certain that there are no problems and that the invoice has been passed to accounts for payment

This is where you start to benefit from the relationship you've developed with your customer's accounts teams. It's amazing the number of times that we've called to check that all is well with an invoice only to find that the invoice has been mislaid (we try to avoid this by printing them on coloured paper, with our logo) or that some query has arisen but no-one's told us about it.

By calling to ask how things are, you may be able to sort out any problems that have arisen and still be paid on time. Make it a rule, then, that first thing every morning your credit controller rings all those companies invoiced seven days previously to check that there are no problems. This method will very quickly highlight problems at your end. Your credit controller will soon start complaining to the dispatch department or the sales team about any problems he's having to deal with, and everyone should pull together to smooth out these blips. As long as you support your credit controller – and everybody knows that you do – you'll benefit in several ways:

- happier customers will buy more from you
- greater sales will result in more cash flowing through the business
- your profits will increase

5. Always send out statements to all outstanding accounts

You'd be surprised by the number of companies that only pay when they receive a statement, so if you don't send them, they will simply forget your invoice. Experience has taught us that a lot of public organisations only pay on statement, but if you work on building a relationship with their accounts depart-ment, you can get payment quicker.

Moving up a gear

So what do you do when the simple rules above don't work? Follow the rules below and stick to the timings suggested.

6. Seven days after the due payment date, phone the debtor and explain that legal action will be taken if payment is not made

It is most important that you make this call. Remind the debtor of your terms of trading and warn that if payment doesn't come within seven days, you won't be able to stop the commencement of legal action.

7. Seven days after that, fill out a writ on a small loans claims form and fax it over, with a note saying that if payment is not received within 14 days, this form will be filed with the small claims court

You will be amazed the effect this has on debtors. They'll ring you up almost immediately and explain that the cheque is on its way, or you'll find out why they can't send it. No-one likes the thought of receiving a writ, and seeing the details in black and white tends to provoke action. This may seem like a radical approach, but remember that you are doing nothing more than sticking to your terms of trade and showing that you intend to get paid.

The beauty of doing this is that you can do it from your office; you don't have to actually go to the court. You simply keep the forms in your office, fill them out and fax them over. Crucially, you don't need to use a solicitor, so you don't incur costs that way.

It's also easy to download these forms from the Internet if you visit **www.courtservice.gov.uk**. When you get to the site, select 'Forms & Guidance' in the left-hand column, then follow the screen prompts for 'County Court' until you reach the forms there. Select 'N1 General Form Part 7' and save it on to your computer as a pdf file. Don't worry if you don't have the Adobe Acrobat Reader program on your computer already (this allows you to view pdf files): you can even download that from the Court Service site.

Countless businesses have been successfully paid, having used this method. It's a simple way of getting hold of money you're owed. There are, of course, occasions where even that doesn't work.

8. If no payment is made, file the writ

If the debtors do not pay, you must then file the writ. The debtors then have 14 days to either file a defence or pay up once and for all. Again, you don't need a solicitor to do this:

you can do it online or by visiting your local county court in person.

If, despite all this, the debtors don't pay, there's only one thing left to do: **take this sum out of your cash flow.**

There is no point to retaining it: it will distort your figures and you must assume that it will not be paid.

NOT ONLY,
BUT ALSO . . .

> If you follow the rules of credit management, your life will be easier and your debtor days will come down. There are further rules that you should also abide by to make debt-chasing easier and your cash flow better.

The first and most important rule is:

1. Always be positive and never prejudge when chasing money

If you need to telephone a late payer, sound positive and confident – even if you don't feel it. Practise beforehand if you need to. If you sound hesitant and apologetic when you call, you won't be treated seriously. The person at the other end will know that you can be put off easily. On the other hand, if you expect a positive outcome rather than the brush-off, your success rate will soar.

For example, we were working with an organisation that was owed a lot of money by a company that had just been taken over. Our clients chased the overdue amount but were told that there was a complete halt on all payments. We were sure that their telephone manner had provoked this response as they had *expected* to be fobbed off, and therefore hadn't gone in positively. We did some Internet research, found out the name of the finance director and called his direct line. He immediately explained that it was correct that there was a stop on new payments, but not on outstanding invoices that had already been presented. To help us, he told us who to call. Of course when we rang the accounts department and mentioned the finance director's name, the payment came out straight away.

The moral? Never assume the response you will get. Go to the top if you can and find out the name of the person in charge and ring him or her direct. Again, you'll get better results if you're positive. The person you speak to you is likely to respond in kind and you'll get the result you want.

2. Stick to these rules!

Any formula for debt-chasing is only successful if you stick to it – and you have to be prepared to follow through. If you say you're going to take action, you must do so, and make sure that errant suppliers are aware of it. They won't take you seriously otherwise.

3. Record the bank details of each of your debtors from their cheques as they come in

Knowing your debtors' bank details can be useful. You will see the benefits of having this information repeatedly.

Set up an address book or card index and record in it each customer's account name and number, bank sort code, contact name, phone number and the name of the person who signs the cheque. This doesn't take long, especially if you make it a habit to check the details at the same time as you or one of your staff fill in the bank paying-in book.

The information will be absolutely essential if, at a later date, you need to freeze their bank account, having got a judgement against them. More importantly than that, it also gives you advance warning of problems. For example, when cheques start coming in from a different bank account, it may mean that the company is having cash-flow problems. On the other hand, they could just have changed their bank, so don't jump to conclusions too quickly.

However, if your customers are individuals rather than businesses, you need to be aware that you must record such data under the terms of the Data Protection Act, which means that you will need a licence to store this information. Visit the Information Commissioner's website for more details: **www.informationcommissioner.gov.uk**.

Bank details can also be useful when you are debt-chasing and are told that there is no-one available to sign the cheque.

It means you can telephone the company, speak to the cheque signatory, and ask her why she isn't signing your cheque. If she says that she doesn't have the final say, you'll be able to explain that you see her signature on every cheque sent out to you normally. You will be surprised by how effective this is, and how often your cheque suddenly arrives.

4. Immediately confirm any agreed changes in payment dates

It's important to record every agreement you make with your customer, so that everyone is clear about next steps and appropriate action. Confirm any phone conversations by e-mail, letter or fax, so that late payers have no excuse to claim that they were unaware of, or had misunderstood, what had been agreed.

5. Keep calm even if others lose their temper

If you have to have a difficult conversation with an errant payer, try as best you can to remain assertive and logical throughout. Once you start shouting, you lose control and you could easily say something you regret, which could ultimately lead to your losing a client. Also, you're much more likely to make sensible decisions when you keep your cool.

6. If the payment delay is due to a failure in *your* organisation, sort it out immediately

You must act quickly if there is a blip in your company's payment systems, or you'll give your client/customer an excuse not to pay.

First, talk to your own accounts team to find and resolve the problem, so that you can be confident that it won't happen again. If you have any conversations with disgruntled customers about the issue, again, make a note of what is said and agreed during that conversation. Write up your notes – a few bullet points are fine – and then email or fax them to the client so that he or she has a record of what each of you are going to do to sort out the situation.

7. Finally, never make empty threats

Everyone wants to avoid the cost and hassle of legal action, but if it's the only resort left to you and you've told the late payer that you're going to take action, be ready to follow through. If you don't, you'll appear weak and the late payer won't take you seriously in future.

10 REVIEWING YOUR TERMS OF TRADE

Why does everyone put 30 days as their terms of trade on their invoices? There's no real reason. These days it should be possible for organisations to pay quicker.

Some do. The Internet has caused a lot to change in this respect. Online enterprises take your order, take your money by credit card, process it and then send the products to you, all automatically. This is how we download music and ring-tones and buy books. If online companies can get paid immediately, why can't more traditional companies benefit in the same way?

You're not legally obliged to give 30 days as your trading terms, but many companies do. In fact, some go further than that and give terms of trade 30 days from the end of the month *following* the date of the invoice. Do you really want to wait that long to get paid?

Thirty days may be standard practice, but it's not obligatory. I suggest that you ask people to pay you within 14 days of the invoice date. Make that change today. And don't worry about doing so – companies *can* pay that quickly. As long as you are crystal clear about these terms when you agree the initial order, it's then up to your credit control department to get the money in. Anyway, even if not *all* your debtors pay within the 14 days, those that do will help your cash flow, so you can't lose.

This chart shows the benefits of changing your terms to 30 days from the date of invoice.

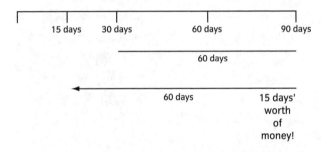

For this illustration, we are assuming that most companies take 60 days to pay an invoice with terms of '30 days from the end of month in which the invoice is raised', and that those companies raise invoices every day throughout the month. This means that if an invoice has been raised on the first of the month, the 30 days doesn't start for another 30 days! As you can see, if your terms were '*30 days from the date of invoice*' you would be paid on that thirtieth day, but no, you have to wait another 30 days!

If you raise invoices regularly over the month, the average date in the month when those invoices are raised will be the fifteenth. Therefore, as soon as you change your terms of trade to '30 days from date of invoice', you immediately bring your money in 15 days earlier.

Changing your terms as described really does work and if you follow the credit-chasing rules in Chapter 8, you'll find that people *will* pay earlier. Let's assume that you go ahead and make this change. You will benefit from 14 extra days' money while at the same time, because you've changed your payment date from 30 to 14 days, you've actually gained a month's cash flow. To show how much this can be, take as an example a company with an annual turnover of £120,000. That company's X figure will be 120,000 divided by 52: £2,308. Therefore, it will be able to put into its bank account that X figure multiplied by four: more than £9,000. How much could *your* company raise?

This is one of the ways that company rescue specialists achieve such dramatic turnarounds with large companies. If a company has a turnover of £120 million, this simple action alone will inject £9 million into the business!

Working with the public sector

Depending on the type of business you have, you may work with public sector bodies, such as local councils. The greatest proportion of their money comes from central government in the form of grants and business rates, which are distributed by the relevant centres on specific days each year. They know exactly how much money they'll have and when it's going to be deposited in their bank account. Don't you dream of a business like that? Wouldn't it make life easier? Of course it would. But despite having all that cash sitting in a bank collecting interest, it can still take them an absolute age to pay you.

Why is that? Certainly bureaucracy is a big hurdle to get over, but there are other elements too. So how can you tackle them? By reducing your credit terms still further. Our educational publishing company supplies schools, so we often deal with local authorities. We found that if we marked our invoices 'due on receipt', the cheques started coming in very quickly – so much so that it made a substantial difference to the cash flow. We found that those schools that paid out of their own accounts paid the invoice almost on the day it arrived, and those invoices paid by the local education authority were sent from the school with an instruction for immediate payment, and we were paid promptly.

Given our success with this, we started suggesting to other companies that they put 'due on receipt' instead of 'within 30 days' on their invoices, and they also began to feel the benefit. This strategy works best with public sector companies, we've found, but it's still worth trying in other sectors. You have nothing to lose.

11
PROTECTING YOURSELF AGAINST SLOW OR NON-PAYING CUSTOMERS

It is always easy to give people credit. It is, however, a banking transaction: *you are lending them money*.

You wouldn't lend money to total strangers in the normal run of things, would you? In business, though, people you've never heard of bowl up and ask you for credit – and you give it to them. Sounds mad, doesn't it? You may argue that it's not that mad really, that you're lending them money to buy your products.

That's an understandable viewpoint, but a loan is still a loan, even if it means that people can buy your products. You are, at this point, simply acting as your customer's banker. If nobody gave credit, companies would still need funds to buy their raw materials before they had sold their end product, and to raise this money they would have to borrow it.

Where from?

A bank.

It is important to realise that you are the banker whenever you give credit. Therefore, you must carry that analogy further and *act* like a bank. Protect yourself by finding out as much as possible about any given company or person before granting them any credit.

You can pay a high price for not doing this research. A small manufacturer of bespoke furniture was asked by a property developer to supply furniture to some plush new apartments. He had been in business for nearly nine years and his customers usually placed orders of between £500 and £1,000. The property developer's order was for more than £20,000. The furniture maker jumped at this chance and did the work without making any checks or finding out anything about his customer. The developer didn't pay and, as a result, the furniture maker had to lay off staff and eventually close down. It was only after the closure that he found that the property developer was not a limited company and had county court judgements (CCJs) totalling more than £33,000 against him. With a record as poor as this, the property developer would have his work cut out getting money from a bank, so where does he go for his funds? To our small, unsuspecting furniture manufacturer!

As you can see, it's crucial that you do your research into anyone placing large orders *before* you do any work for them. You may even come across seemingly respectable customers who buy a few low-value products from you, pay promptly, and then place a much larger order. By this time you feel that you have got to know them and built up a good working relationship, so you take the order, only for them not to pay the larger than usual invoice. The key thing is not to get carried away by the size of an order. It is, of course, very tempting to indulge in some daydreams – thinking about how it will change your company, allow you to expand as planned, and so on – but don't let it go so far that you become scared of losing the work and forget that you were doing fine before it came along. Check out your new star customer's credit rating first . . . *then* celebrate!

Credit ratings

It's easy to get a credit check done. You can approach the potential customer's bank for a reference, but these tend to be rather vague. Trade references are also, in my opinion, not worth staking your house on: it's highly unlikely that your prospective customer is going to give you the name of a company that he or she has a bad credit history with. Rather, you'll be put in touch with somebody who is paid promptly. So if you can't completely rely on trade references, whom can you trust?

It's a good idea to visit the Companies House website at **www.companies-house.gov.uk** where for only a few pounds, you can buy a set of the latest accounts and details of every limited company registered in the UK. From these figures, you can work out their X figure (see Chapter 2 for a refresher) and use this to calculate their debtor, creditor and stock days. You can quickly learn how well a company is doing and how long they take to pay their creditors. Also, because the accounts show you the previous year's figures, you should be able to see trends and tell if the company has been going through a rough patch.

To bear in mind

You want figures that are as up to date as possible. Ideally, you want figures that have just been filed. Unfortunately, it's not that simple to get hold of these, as companies have eight months from the end of their financial year to file their accounts. This means that if you look at a company in July with a September year-end, the accounts you are looking at will be not for the year that ended last September, but the one that ended 21 months ago, and a lot can happen to a company in 21 months.

On balance, though, Companies House is probably the most

reliable source of the figures you want. Recently we worked with a company that had grown very quickly. The managing director told me that they couldn't have grown that quickly if they hadn't kept their creditors happy. A reasonable comment, but the other way to look at it is that they could only have funded such growth with their creditors' money. So I checked their accounts at Companies House and found out that I was right: they had used their creditors to fund growth and regularly paid their creditors within an average of 90 days. I went back and explained to the managing director that, as a small company, we couldn't do business in this way. We ended up with an agreement that he would pay us within 14 days, which he did.

So how do we get around the problem of filed accounts being historical? You use a credit agency, which can give you a credit assessment on a company very quickly. One such company is First Report. You can contact them online or by fax. You buy, in advance, a series of credit requests and in return are sent the relevant forms. Every time you need a fast credit check, fill in the form with the company name or registration number, tick the boxes for the information you require and fax it over. Normally it comes back within about 10 minutes, with the information we requested, including a credit rating for that company. It is a very quick and simple service that has saved us many thousands of pounds and, more importantly, many sleepless nights.

There are several other companies offering this service. With most you buy a certain number of credit requests in advance. For example, if you visit the Credit@ssist website (**www.creditassist.co.uk**), you can enter a company's name and registration number and their credit details will be sent back to your desktop immediately. A credit check will cost you less than £15, so there's no excuse not to make use of a service of this type.

You may wonder how these companies are able to give you an up-to-date credit reference. Well, obviously they use Companies House. They then check for county court judgements, and many of them are also linked to Dun & Bradstreet, the biggest credit reference agency in the world. Dun & Bradstreet have a very clever system that allows them to keep a check on whether a company's debtors and creditors are growing or reducing. For example, if a company is extending its creditors, it could be that they are having difficulty in paying their debts, which means that one should be careful. Dun & Bradstreet have refined this system further by calculating the average number of creditor days within each business sector, so that you can see how a specific company is operating within its particular sector.

Therefore, it is essential that you use a credit reference agency for all your larger debtors and every new company to which you offer credit. It will save you more than it costs you.

Bouncing cheques

Bad cheques happen to good people, sadly. It is possible to insure against them, though, and there are several routes you could go down.

- **Transax** is the largest debt insurer. They are good but expensive, so look at your margins and see what you can afford before you go any further. Some banks, such as Barclays, offer Transax protection.
- **Trade Indemnity** (020 7860 8060) will also insure your debts, but are also expensive. Whether you use them or not will probably depend on the number of bad debts you get in your particular industry.

> Consider this issue carefully. You may get so annoyed by bad cheques and companies failing on you that you start looking for protection against bad debt. Don't forget that it will cost you money to take out this protection. Before you insure your debts, check that the amount you pay out for this insurance is *not* more than your provision for bad debts.

There are other simple ways to protect yourself. For example, it is always a good idea to add a **retention of title** clause to your terms of trade. This clause means that you retain ownership of any goods you supply until payment is made. A lot of people are cynical about these clauses, but they can work. You must show, when you try to enforce the clause, that your customer knew of it, which is why it should always be on the face of the invoice. If you can get a signature from the customer on a letter you sent alerting him or her to the existence of the clause, then your case is even stronger.

The problem with such clauses is that in a court of law, defendants can claim that they never knew about the clause. Unless you can prove to the court's satisfaction that they did, you're unlikely to win. In truth, a retention of title clause only really comes into play in a liquidation case. In these circumstances, you will want to get your product back as soon as possible. Therefore, as soon as you hear of the liquidation, contact the liquidators and tell them about the clause. They will almost certainly be in the middle of an enormous muddle that needs sorting out quickly, in order that they can present some figures to the creditors' meeting. If you can catch them at this point with a clear and lucid argument – you have a retention of title clause and a signature acknowledging it – they may decide to let you take your goods back.

Also, don't forget some useful late payment legislation which states:

'All small businesses, with 50 or fewer employees, can use the rights given to them by the Late Payment of

Commercial Debts (Interest) Act 1998 to claim interest
retrospectively.'

The late payment interest rate that applies in the UK is calculated as the reference rate plus 8%. The reference rate is
the Bank of England base rate on either 31 December or
30 June in any given year, depending on which date is
nearer. For example, the reference rate charged in May 2006
was the base rate of 4.5%, plus 8%, giving 12.5%.

Charge the late payment interest rate on late invoices, if
you can. It's not necessarily practical, though, in that you run
the risk of losing most of your customers. You can, however,
use it as a warning, and make certain that you always add it
when you go to court.

It is important to note this little clause in the legislation:

'Please also note that businesses with their own contract
terms for late payment interest forfeit their right to use
the late payment legislation.'

The good thing about this is that it is statutory, so if
they don't pay you it doesn't have to be in your terms and
conditions for you to be able to charge it.

Debt collection agencies

Let's assume you have a lot of bad debts, and that you've
tried all legal routes to get your money but nothing has

worked. You get a cold call from a debt collection agency. Divine intervention? Maybe, maybe not. If you do decide to go down this route, take care and follow these rules:

- *never* pay a fee in advance
- always confirm *when* the collected debt will be paid over to you
- check the reputation of the agency with your local Trading Standards Office
- never sign anything on the first meeting
- be wary of the 'satisfied' customers offered as references – they may indeed be genuine, but you have no way of knowing
- send them away if they claim that they are 'insurance backed', so that if they don't get the money, their insurance company will pay out. This simply isn't true. *No* insurance company offers such cover to a debt collection agency.

It is worth following these rules, as the only debts you are going to give them are old ones that you can't collect. The problem is that once you hand them over to a debt collection agency they can still cost you. Think carefully and make sure that you don't throw good money after bad.

12
WORKING SUCCESSFULLY WITH CREDITORS

Previous chapters have focused on how you can put cash into your business by reducing debtor weeks. Another effective way of improving your cash business is by increasing your creditor weeks – that is, how long it takes you to pay others.

Keep talking

Remember: you're both a debtor and a creditor. When you're talking to your own creditors, ask yourself, 'If I were told this, would I believe it?' If you wouldn't believe it, why should they?

We discussed the short-term panic problem in Chapter 5. It's one that affects most small businesses at one point or another, but the way you deal with the issue when it hits your business will set the tone for the future of the company. If you handle it well, your business will survive and prosper.

In the short term, your problem is that you can't pay your creditors because you don't have the money to do so.

Whatever you do, don't avoid the issue or the people you owe money to. To keep them on side, talk to them regularly and honestly. Most people do exactly the opposite and try to avoid their creditors until they have the money to pay them. This never works. Why not? Because, as we said earlier, you are both a debtor and a creditor. You have debtors; in fact it is probably because those debtors haven't paid you that you are in this position in the first place. When your debtors don't talk to you, what do you think? You get jittery and start imagining that you are going to lose your money. You worry so much that eventually you decide that, no matter what happens, you will never get it and start taking drastic action.

To get things back on track, break the cycle. Take the initiative to contact your creditors. Call them as soon as you know that you have a problem, explain the situation and how you intend to sort it out, and then give them a realistic date when they can expect payment.

This will surprise your creditor – in a good way. Someone has actually phoned to explain why a cheque isn't coming before he or she had even started to chase it. Wow! You are gaining Brownie points, and this should give you the breathing space you need to sort out your short-term cash position.

Having lived through many cash-flow crises over many years, we have learned that keeping creditors informed of progress means that they normally support us. It isn't just that they are nice people, but because once your debt is on their sales ledger they become very reluctant to admit that it won't be settled: they've probably already spent that money somewhere else on the assumption that it will be paid. Keeping everyone in the loop, then, helps settle nerves on all sides.

You still can't pay . . . but keep talking

OK. You weren't able to pay. Your creditors gave you a welcome extension. What happens when the day arrives when you said you'd pay, but you still don't have the money? Again, call and tell them. They will still stay with you – if for no other reason than they're locked in and need the money from you – but you will have damaged your credibility and that will take time to rebuild.

This is only a short-term solution, but what you really want is a long-term way to stretch your creditors out, so you don't have to pay for anything until you get paid yourself. This would be the ideal solution, as the best way to fund your business is on the back of your creditors. To be able to pay suppliers after *you* have been paid means that you won't have a cash-flow problem, and that your creditors will fund the growth of your business.

Charles Dunstone – who built Carphone Warehouse into a billion-pound business – is on record as saying, 'You have to be a good partner to your supplier. Starting up, I think that was the greatest lesson I learned. We basically funded our business by using our suppliers' cash flow in that we sold goods before we had to pay for them'. He went on to say, 'suppliers are the cheapest working capital you'll ever get', and his massive success is a testament to it. So you need to get your creditors to fund your business, and to do that you must talk to them. You must build up a good relationship with them so that you're in a position to negotiate payment terms that give you time to sell your stock *before* you have to pay for it. That is how the company I talked about in Chapter 11 had grown so quickly, and why they paid their creditors in 90 days. It allowed them to get paid well before they needed to pay their suppliers.

So how do you do this? The most obvious way is to negotiate long-term payments with your suppliers. If you are Carphone Warehouse, people come into your shops and pay as they purchase. They actually started as a mail-order business, which also meant that they were paid before they shipped the goods and probably, in the beginning, only ordered stock when they got an order themselves.

That's the theory. In practice, it's quite difficult to pull off. If you run a traditional retail business, you have to stock your shop with product, and most of it won't move that quickly. In such circumstances you need to get as much stock as you can on a sale or return basis, which again will help your cash flow.

The most obvious example of this approach is the book trade, where most chains expect to get their books on sale or return. If you can't do this – and most of us can't – you need to negotiate longer credit terms with your suppliers. If you do this from a position of strength, and are buying regularly from them, you will be surprised by how often suppliers are receptive to this idea.

At the same time, start extending your payment dates. Do it *slowly*. You will find a lot of creditors don't chase, which means that you may be able to spread your creditors out a week at a time. If creditors chase you, always pay them on the due date but you'll be surprised by how few of them will notice. When you are chased, simply note the date and how long it was after the invoice was raised, and record that as the date for future payments to that creditor.

At the same time, look at each individual creditor invoice and the terms of trade relating to it. Look closely at the date they specify for payment. Can't find it? Don't be surprised: many companies put lots of information on their invoices, but forget to say when they want to be paid. Seriously, it's true – go and look.

Now relate all these invoices to the dates when you actually pay them. You will probably find this is at the end of the month following receipt: if you receive an invoice on 10 April, then, you don't need to pay until 31 May. For those invoices without a due date you can legitimately delay payment, but do this slowly. Start by delaying payment by just one week, then if they don't scream or even notice, slip it by another week, and after a few months you will have got that extra month.

You will learn from doing this how few people chase a debt that slips slowly to 90 days, and how many will accept it when you say that these are your standard terms. The rule is to make certain that those terms are on your standard purchase order and on the invoice when it arrives. Therefore, naturally, the next thing you need to do is to change the standard terms of trade on your purchase orders to 90 days from end of month of invoice. Again you will be taken aback by how few people read these terms of trade, simply because they are so pleased to get the order.

If a supplier baulks at this, don't argue: simply agree a different payment date with him or her. Again, it will surprise you how many suppliers will accept your terms of trade and, also, how many of them, when they baulk at these terms, will settle on 60 days and still not chase you until 90 days – which is what you wanted anyway!

When you go through your suppliers' invoices, put aside all the factored ones. As we saw earlier, you want as many of these as you can. You can tell them because they are the invoices that tell you to pay a different company. There is normally a clause stamped on the front of the invoice assigning it to somebody else.

Put all these aside and make a note to pay them all after 88 days. Earlier, when explaining factoring, I said that the factor charges interest for the time between paying and receiving payment and it is therefore not to his benefit for you to pay promptly. If you are a client who pays on the eighty-ninth day, you'll be popular, as they're making money out of you.

You can't drag the payment date out beyond 90 days, as most factoring companies have a clause returning the invoice if the client hasn't paid within 90 days.

Now that you know which of your suppliers you can delay, and those that need prompt payment, you can move to the next stage, which is to set up a system to pay your suppliers only on two dates each month.

Again you must keep your suppliers informed, so send them a letter telling them when the payment dates will be. You must also give a valid reason for this change, which is normally that it is due to your new computer system and goes something like this:

'We are pleased to tell you that we have installed a new computer system to improve the efficiency of our financial operation. This requires specific debtor and creditor input days, giving a more efficient payment system resulting in specific dates for the raising of cheques. Therefore, to allow you to benefit from our improved system by knowing exactly when your cheque will arrive, payment runs will be made twice a month on the fifteenth and thirtieth days of the month.'

I am sure you have received many similar letters to this and that you, like 90% of other suppliers, accept them. For the 10% that don't, make an exception but in doing so make sure they know you're doing something out of the ordinary for them. They will then feel special, which means that if you do have any problem with their product or service, you know that they will correct it quickly because they won't want to damage this important relationship.

The most important rule to remember when extending your creditor days is that you must do it *while* keeping your creditors happy. The good news is how few of them actually check payment dates.

13
CONTROLLING STOCK

Stock is another area of the business that eats up your cash, so much so that sometimes I call it 'dead money'. Why? Because once you've invested your hard-earned cash in stock, that money is not available to you until the stock has been sold and paid for and the proceeds safely banked.

Stock turn

If you sell any type of product, your business will need stock. Stock is what makes you money, and therefore the more you sell and replace it, the more money you make. This cash movement is called 'stock turn'.

To illustrate, let's assume that you buy £1,000 worth of stock. You sell it within a week for £2,000. The following week, you buy another £1,000 worth of stock with your original £1,000 and during that week you sell it for a further £2,000.

In two weeks, your original £1,000 has made you £2,000, and in those two weeks you have turned your stock over twice. Continue doing this for a year and you will have turned your stock over 52 times. The money tied up in stock will be two weeks and, most importantly, you will have made £52,000 from only a £1,000 outlay.

On the other hand, if you spend £1,000 on stock that takes six months to sell for £2,000, you have only turned your stock over twice in a year, and your initial outlay has only made you £2,000 during a whole year. Therefore, if you turn your stock over just twice a year and you want to make £52,000 in that year, you will need to make an investment of £26,000.

As we said earlier, stock is an essential part of any business – we all need it. The problem is that as soon as it's created, it starts to lose money unless you move it. Imagine it as piles of £10 notes which could easily blow away in the wind unless you protect them. This image is a very apt one: if you don't look after stock and keep it in pristine condition, you won't be able to sell it. As it deteriorates, so does its value. If the stock in your business has a shelf life – if you run a café or a greengrocer's shop, say – you need to be especially vigilant.

Sometimes people can't bear to let stock go. If they've spent a lot of time choosing it, for example, then they feel very proprietorial towards it and can't look at the situation rationally. You must take a step back, though, and realise that the mountain of stuff won't go anywhere unless you take active steps to move it.

Moving 'dead' stock

Let's assume that you identify £10,000 worth of slow-moving stock. It has been sitting there for six months. This means that your investment has failed to make you any money for six months, and yet it is still occupying space in your warehouse, doing nothing. Ever the optimist, you feel that it's a good-quality item and that you'll make a lot of money from it when you eventually find a buyer.

That's fair enough, but what if you don't find this magical buyer? Could you have made even more money by spending it on different stock? For example, what would happen if you dumped the lacklustre stock at 50% of what you paid for it, and put that money into buying faster-moving stock? Would it make you more money?

As an illustration, take a piece of paper. At the top, write £10,000 – let's assume this is part of your slow-moving stock. For the purposes of this exercise, sell the stock for 50% of its value – £5,000. You should be able to do that pretty quickly. Yes, I know you think it's worth much more than that, but it simply isn't while it's just lurking in your warehouse. Now, underneath the £10,000 write £5,000. On our sheet of paper this £5,000 is now going to buy some fast-moving stock which will be sold within a month, giving a profit of 20%, or £1,000.

With this paper exercise, during Month One our original £10,000 has made us £1,000, whereas the actual £10,000 worth of stock sitting in your warehouse has made you nothing.

Over the next six months, if we keep reinvesting that £5,000 in the same stock we will make £6,000, when in those same six months our original investment of £10,000 has made nothing. Therefore, in this exercise, the original £10,000 worth of stock that we dumped at 50% is now, in effect, worth £11,000, making us £1,000. Over the next six months this £10,000 could go on to make us a further £6,000. And this money can be made simply by dumping your stock at 50% of its buying price.

That's why you need to sell dead stock as quickly as possible. Think about the January sales: it's an opportunity for the big stores to dump stock and use that money to earn more with new, faster-moving items. If they can do it, so can you. Review your stock levels continually – and ruthlessly – and if the stock isn't moving quickly enough, dump it and use the money to buy or create items that will.

At this point it is worth noting that when banks take a debenture as being 'a full and floating charge' over your business and its assets, they only include your stock at 10% of its valuation. I think this shows very clearly how easy it is for your stock to lose value.

Innovate

Find as many different ways as possible to keep your stock down. Be innovative. For example, we recently worked with a publisher of technical manuals who had just moved into a new warehouse. His company was growing quickly and as a result he needed to find ever more storage space for his stock. His target market couldn't get enough of his technical manuals, so he extended his product range. In one sense, then, his success was a dream come true, but in another sense it was a nightmare: each time the company published a new manual, they had to print a minimum of 5,000 copies to get a competitive price. The books were then stored in the warehouse. Because he was offering a wider range of books all the time, when I visited him he had over £1 million worth of stock in storage. The company was doing well on paper, but they were running out of space and the amount of money tied up in stock was beginning to affect their cash flow.

So what was the solution? We suggested that rather than print 5,000 copies of each publication, he invest in a state-of-the-art digital printing system. This was a large outlay and meant that the unit cost of the books would rise, but it also meant that once the system was up and running, each time a customer placed an order, the staff could simply press a button on the computer. It would then print out a specially bound copy of the manual and all they would need to do was dispatch it.

The new machinery would reduce the amount of cash paid out in renting warehouse space, and therefore also cut down on staff costs. Over time, as the business sold the pile of existing manuals, the money tied up in stock would move to the bank account and become real money. This money would give the company positive cash flow and eventually put an extra £1 million into the business. The extra money gained would more than compensate for the increased unit cost of the manuals.

Have I convinced you? I hope so. The next step is to clear out your slow-moving stock. How do you do it? The first obvious way is to have a sale. People can't resist a bargain – just look at the queues outside large department stores after Christmas. Tap into this, then, and offer your stock to customers at 'sale' prices. One company I know always have an auctioneer at their annual sale. He carries out a proper auction, which makes certain that all stock is cleared while giving their customers the chance to get a bargain.

If sales don't grab you, you could also try:

■ **eBay.** On this successful website you can sell anything, which offers you a simple way of clearing unwanted stock. In fact, anybody can set up a store within the site. For example, a friend of ours with a record company has his own store on eBay. Originally, he planned to use it to clear dead stock, but it has become so successful that he puts new CDs on there and sells them at his list price successfully. He loves the eBay route because everyone pays through PayPal, which means his money is safe *and* he gets paid quickly.

- **auction houses.** Most towns have auctioneers who will take your stock and sell it at their weekly or monthly auction.

- **market traders** are another useful way to clear out your stock, or you can use auction magazines like *Exchange & Mart* (which also has an online presence at **www.exchangeandmart.co.uk**).

- **your own website**, if you have one, and come up with some attractive special offers.

- **advertising** in the local newspaper.

Once you have reduced your stock turn, you need a system that ensures that your stock levels don't slowly start to creep back up again. You must therefore put in place a system that allows you to continually monitor the stock position. The easiest way to do this is to relate your stock to 'stock weeks' (turn back to Chapter 2 if you need to refresh your memory). To start with, check your stock on a weekly basis, so that you can take into account the rise and fall of your sales.

Change the way you buy

It's important to scrutinise closely how you buy your stock. Chart your purchases and work out how much you buy at a time. For example, your suppliers probably give you a discount for bulk purchases. Is it really to your benefit to tie up so much capital by buying in bulk? Work out whether you could actually make a greater profit by buying on a 'just-in-time' basis, just as the technical publisher did.

Naturally your suppliers will want you to buy in bulk, as it gives them orders in advance and they get their money faster. But if you negotiate with them, you should be able to agree a 'just-in-time' contract. Do make absolutely sure that this contract will definitely benefit you: work out how much you need each day or each week – whichever is more appropriate for your business – and then arrange for your supply to come on that basis. You now explain that you expect the same prices as for a bulk order as this is in effect what you are giving your supplier. It *is* still a bulk order – but one that is to be delivered over a period of time on a regular basis. This will benefit your supplier, who will now have a regular order that helps with their own ordering and production planning.

When you approach your supplier, don't feel that you're doing so from a position of weakness. Remember that this is a mutually beneficial arrangement and, as long as you are positive when you suggest it, you'll find that you could get even better terms from your supplier. Try it and see what happens.

A big warning

Be very careful when you agree a regular delivery and be sure to think through all the implications extremely carefully before you proceed. Consider this story about a man who had a small electrical business. He was good at his job, the work was regular, his customers liked him and, best of all, he was making good money. Then one day he said to himself, 'While I'm travelling to jobs, why don't I sell a few bits and pieces like light bulbs, timer switches and fans?' He went out and bought some goods cheaply and put a small display in the back of the van. The problem was that to get a good price, he had to agree to take a regular shipment. This sounded fine at first, but life became more difficult when the items didn't sell as quickly as he'd hoped, while he still had to take regular deliveries of them. The electrician ended up taking a stall in the market to sell the goods, which meant that he wasn't spending as much time as he should on his electrical jobs. His income fell, his debts increased, and the goods kept coming through the door. The problem was that he couldn't sell enough to make the same money he had as an electrician, or to pay for the stock that was piling up.

In short, then, never agree a regular supply unless you know that you can sell the products in question. If you are currently buying in bulk, it should be simple to work out a 'just-in-time' delivery programme, as you know your sales pattern. Don't do it for new products simply because you *think* they will sell. But whatever happens, when you agree a just-in-time supply contract, make certain that there is a way you can get out of it.

Again, the key message is: *keep in touch*. If our electrician had done so and not been frightened about going to see his supplier, there would have been a very good chance that his supplier would have agreed to change the order or delivery schedule. After all, suppliers don't want to sell products that won't sell on to someone else. They need to get paid for what they ship, and if their customers can't pay them, there's no point dispatching something that will only become a bad debt. If the supplier had wanted to lose money that badly, he could just as easily have torn up £10 notes for all the good it did him.

As ever, communication is key: if you have a problem, talk to someone about it before it gets out of hand.

Faulty goods

Right, so we have a tight rein on the stock position, but our stock is still growing. What's going on? There are many potential explanations, of course, but one of the most obvious is that your pile of faulty goods is growing.

As a good business that looks after its customers, when one of your customer returns faulty goods, naturally you take them back and issue a replacement. But what happens to those faulty goods? They go back into stock. Every time you replace faulty goods, you are increasing your stock. It's essential, then, that you keep on top of this situation before it bleeds you dry.

If a customer buys goods that turn out not to be fit for the purpose for which they were supplied, you must replace them under the Sale of Goods Act (the DTI website has a useful factsheet on it). If you sold an unfit product, it is your fault, but usually it will be because your supplier has provided you with faulty goods in the first place. Therefore, it is important that you have an agreement with that supplier to replace faulty goods without penalising you.

A lot of companies offer this, but not many carry it out in practice. It costs them money to replace that faulty stock, so they stall you, coming up with all kinds of excuses, from waiting for the testing department to get back to them, to a delay with their supplier. It is vital that you watch out for this and make certain that you are credited promptly for all faulty goods.

Make it a rule that you always return faulty goods with an invoice. This gives you a benchmark, allowing you to keep a check of the position and to relate the value of faulty goods to your outstanding debt with that supplier. This money should be credited from your debt to him, but in most cases it isn't. Suppliers do not like doing this and will therefore always query such invoices, but you must remember that unless the goods are credited, you will suffer, and you've had enough hassle already because what you bought wasn't up to scratch.

In the late 1980s and early 1990s there was a boom in the number of small computer manufacturers. There were literally hundreds, most of whom eventually went bust. They were making money, but went bust because their stock levels grew too high too quickly. Now some of these businesses were even large public companies, but they still went bust.

How did this happen? All these companies were building computers from components bought from component suppliers in the Far East. It was a cash business. The computers were sold for cash, the components were bought from the suppliers for cash and the importers paid in cash. It was also a just-in-time business, so everybody kept stock levels very low. In theory, everybody should have made lots of money. But there is a big difference between theory and practice.

The problem lay in the quality of the components. They were being built so quickly that quality control was low. In a sense, this wasn't a problem, because the manufacturers would replace them, but another problem compounded the situation: their incompatibility with other components. This was a business where Intel, the chip manufacturer, was very proud of the fact that they doubled the speed of their CPU –

the computer's 'brain' – every two years. This meant that if the brain was doubling in speed every other year, all other components had to as well, and this is what led to the problems. Add to this the fact that it was a time when *everybody* was buying a computer. Bill Gates of Microsoft had the vision of a computer on every desk and it was happening as he'd predicted; orders were coming in at an amazing rate.

So fast, in fact, that most computers were being built and shipped out *on the same day*. Theoretically, this was a perfect way to keep stock turning over quickly. Here was a cash business, with high turnover, low margins and little stock. So why did it go so wrong for so many people? Because the stock on everyone's balance sheets just kept on rising. As the stock went up, the available cash in the businesses came down. This happened because as all these new computers were being built on the production line, if a component failed, the manufacturer would pick up another one – which *did* work – and put it into the computer. The faulty component was then sent back to the supplier. Of course the manufacturer needed a replacement, so he bought another for cash. Sales were coming in so fast that he had to build as many computers as he could, as fast as he could, which meant that he had to order replacement parts before his supplier had replaced the faulty ones. The supplier would test the board and send it back to the Far East, and would then get a replacement, which he then sent to the manufacturer. All this could take as long as three months, during which time the computer manufacturer had to buy new components.

The result was that he was building up further stocks of faulty components that were sitting on his balance sheet until they were replaced, which meant that, while he had no stock in his warehouse, on his balance sheet his stock was rising. Add to this the fact that all suppliers required payment on delivery, and our computer manufacturer was beginning to run out of money.

Then, to make life worse, as more and more components were being made, the benefits of scale started to kick in. This meant that each month the price of his components was falling. Now our computer manufacturer was getting into even more financial trouble as, even though his components were being replaced like for like, the price was lower each time.

This meant that the faulty parts being held in stock were being replaced with ones worth less. Therefore, on a regular basis the manufacturer had to write down the value of perfectly good stock. A nightmare!

This is a classic case of profitable companies running out of money and it can happen to large public companies as well as small ones. In one year in the early 1990s I counted six public companies in the computer market that went under, all because of the same problem. So take care: if your stock is rising and you can't work out why, look at your position with regard to faulty stock.

14

THE 10% RULE

In 1992, Nigel Mansell became the Formula 1 world champion. It was also the year in which he was sacked by Williams, the team for which he was driving.

That was a hard decision for Williams to make, but there was a good business reason for it. Nigel Mansell was being paid a retainer of several million pounds by the Williams team, and his clinching of the world championship meant that it was going to increase yet again. Sir Frank Williams, the team boss, realised that this could push his team into making a loss and knew that if he could sign up Alain Prost, a previous world champion, for less, he could save his company several millions. The business would stay in profit, and with a driver of Prost's calibre he would still have a chance of winning the next world championship and keeping his sponsors happy. This is exactly what he did. Expenses were reduced, profits stayed stable and the team kept winning – and, indeed, his team won the world championship again. So it can be done.

This is an unusual example, but a good illustration of a key principle of effective cash management: you increase the amount of money in your business when you reduce what you spend on expenses. As a result, you'll be able to reduce the amount of money that your business needs to make each day if it is to survive.

Before you can reduce expenses effectively, you need to know exactly what they are.

Analysing expenses

To start off your analysis, split up your expenses into the following key areas:

- fixed expenses
- variable expenses
- cost of sales

Fixed expenses are the costs of running your business before you sell anything. They will include your staff costs, premises costs, utility bills, direct debits, and so on. These costs are roughly the same every month.

Variable expenses are those expenses that fluctuate due to production and the levels of your sales. They include items such as sales commission, petrol, motor expenses, your reps' mobile phone bills, and so on.

Cost of sales encompasses all the costs incurred in

creating and selling the goods or services your business offers. This includes items such as materials, labour, advertising, marketing, and so on.

All of these costs can be trimmed. As a rule of thumb, if you can reduce each of your expenses and your cost of sales by 10%, your profits rise by more than 10%. For example, Smith & Jones Ltd has a turnover of £100,000, a 30% gross profit margin and is making £5,000 profit:

Turnover		£100,000
Cost of sales	£70,000	
Expenses	£25,000	£ 95,000
Net profit		£ 5,000

If both expenses and cost of sales are reduced by 10%, the costs look quite different:

Turnover		£100,000
Cost of sales	£63,000	
Expenses	£22,500	£ 85,500
Net profit		£ 14,500

A 10% reduction in both increases profits almost three times as much.

Apply this principle to your own business, and see what impact it could have.

Cutting expenditure

Cutting back on what you pay out is a key part of the 10% rule, so take some time to look at every single expenditure made by your company. It will be time well spent. Finding the first savings is often the most difficult stage, but once you get into this way of thinking, it gradually becomes easier to find ways to save.

Every single saving will help, no matter how small. A saving of £10 a week will become £40 a month, and that translates into nearly £500 over a year. Whatever type of business you're in, all those little expenses can build up to make substantial savings. For example, when Philip Green took over BHS, he found a more efficient method of producing and labelling coat hangers, which meant that each one was a penny cheaper. As BHS uses so many coat hangers, they ended up saving £400,000. Obviously small businesses don't have access to this scale of reduction, but you can see the principle behind it.

When you set up a business, many people start off in a room at home or a small office somewhere. Your expenses are quite small then, but they have a tendency to grow over time. Unless you keep them in check, they'll grow out of all proportion. The problem is that every day decisions have to be made and each one is an excuse to spend money. I use the word 'excuse', because the *Oxford English Dictionary* defines 'excuse' as: 'to seek or serve to justify'. It is true that, subconsciously, we always find ourselves justifying our expenditure. The key rule to bear in mind is this: don't spend *unless* that expenditure will help your business reach its goals.

To illustrate, in the 1920s, the aviator Charles Lindbergh was preparing to make his historic flight from New York to Paris. In the planning stage, he had to make exactly the same decisions as if he were running a business. He had to decide what to take with him; there were a lot of things that he felt he needed, and even more that everybody thought he could do with. These items fell into two categories:

1. Those that would make his journey more comfortable.
2. Those that would increase his chances of reaching his target (Paris).

For example, weight was a real problem. Lindbergh had a choice. He could take petrol with him, which would increase his safety, or he could take a compass, which would increase his chances of finding and eventually reaching Paris. Whenever he was faced with a decision of this type, he always chose the solution that would increase his chances of reaching Paris, rather than one that would increase his comfort. As we know, his journey was a great success, so why not apply this rule to your own business?

The office

Businesses spend a vast amount of money on their office space.

Parkinson's Law, or The Pursuit of Progress, written in 1957 by the late Professor C. Northcote Parkinson, states that 'Dynamic and creative organisations are found in temporary huts or overcrowded offices bulging at the seams with make-do furniture and equipment. Once an organisation achieves the perfect headquarters it is probably well into terminal decline.'

It's so true. While you obviously need to make sure that your premises are safe, hygienic and appropriate for the work being carried out in them, going over the top with designer furniture and fittings won't help you meet your business goals. Your cash would be better off in your bank account, working hard for the business.

I saw this point illustrated first-hand 20 years ago. At the time, I owned an office equipment company in the West Midlands, and we were contracted to supply the De Lorean car factory in Northern Ireland as well as the buying office in Coventry. John De Lorean was a former director of General Motors who had a dream of building a sports car with gull-wing doors: the design was a real 1980s icon. He convinced the British government that his idea was a good one, that the cars would sell by the million and that manufacturing them would be the perfect way to reduce unemployment in Northern Ireland. Millions of pounds of public money was invested in the project.

One day I was summoned to the Coventry office, where the team showed me a wall opposite the lift that was painted a lovely shade of light blue. It appeared that Mr De Lorean was appalled that it had nothing on it. He said that it didn't reflect the image of a major sports car manufacturer and he wanted a photograph of the car that covered the whole wall on a solid wooden base with an ornate frame, so that as people came out of the lift they felt they had arrived at the offices of a major organisation.

There was no way such a picture could be carried in. The lift was too small, as were the stairs. The painting could be assembled *in situ*, though, which was expensive. We were instructed to go ahead, but he wanted to see it within a week, which cost even more. Again we obliged (why wouldn't we? he was paying). Finally, everything was ready for the arrival of the great man. After his visit we received a message saying he didn't want it and they would pay us to take it out. How did that decision help the De Lorean Motor Company to reach its goal?

This wasn't a one-off. There was vast expenditure on comfort, but hardly anything spent on reaching their goal of producing a car and selling it. I understand that the walls of De Lorean's New York offices were lined with famous art treasures. How did that help? Is it any wonder that the company failed?

Professor Parkinson was spot on. Whenever you're tempted to spend money, follow Lindbergh's example and ask yourself, 'Will this expenditure increase our chances of reaching our goal?'

The Ryanair way

Looking for ways of reducing your expenses is a habit you need to get into. The best way to do this is to look at your business as if you were an outsider. Challenge the status quo and be prepared to take a fresh look at all aspects. Cultivate the right mindset and continually ask yourself whether each individual expenditure will increase your comfort or increase your chances of reaching your goal. If it's the former, don't go there. As you continue to search, you'll find that looking for 10% becomes easier and easier.

One of the most famous examples of this approach is Ryanair. In June 2004 they reported an annual profit of £226 million on a turnover of £1,074 million; for the same period, British Airways showed a profit of £230 million on a turnover of £7.65 billion. BA clearly fly on longer and more varied routes than Ryanair, but just think of how much profit they could make if they adopted Ryanair's entrepreneurial spirit.

One major reason why Ryanair's costs are so much lower is that you can only buy tickets for their flights online, which means that there's no need for a call centre or for the company to pay commission to travel agents. British Airways are making some moves in a similar direction, but are still selling through travel agents at the moment. This is what happens to a company that has been doing something for many years. It becomes reluctant to remodel and inevitably finds reasons not to make those necessary changes. You will usually find that it is the older company that has the greater expenses, while it is the newer, faster-growing, hungrier one that has the lowest expenses.

You see an illustration of this when you look at the number of hours flown by a Ryanair pilot, as opposed to those flown by a BA pilot. As a result of many years' negotiations between British Airways and BALPA, the pilots' union, their pilots now only fly up to 650 hours a year, while Ryanair's fly between 800 and 850 hours a year. This is a heavy workload, but one still within the safety limit set by the Civil Aviation Authority of 900 hours. The result, of course, is that the new boy, Ryanair, is getting 30% more flights out of each pilot, meaning that for the same number of flights they need 30% fewer pilots – an enormous saving in salaries for the highest-paid members of staff.

It's good to talk . . .

Let's look at obvious areas and start with something as mundane as your telephone bill. Did you know that over 70% of all businesses still pay a minimum call charge? Telephone companies charge you for every call you make, whether it takes 10 seconds or two minutes – if the person you want isn't there and you put the phone down, you'll still be charged. For some reason, businesses tend to overlook this, probably because they're focusing on larger savings to be made elsewhere. That's all well and good, but it's worth examining the smaller details, in case they represent an opportunity to put money back into your business in some other, more useful way.

Get into the habit of checking your phone bill (all bills, in fact) regularly. It really will pay off. We spend a lot of time on the phone in our business and as a result we only use telephone companies that don't impose a minimum call charge. One day our bill arrived and it was nearly double that of the previous month. We looked at the call log on the bill and noticed that a minimum charge had been instituted. Perplexed, I called the financial director of the company we dealt with and explained the situation. He apologised, agreed that we had a contract and said that he would issue a credit that day.

When we got the next statement, there was the credit. I called to thank him, and had a surprising conversation. He explained that they had decided to put the minimum charge on everyone's bill and wait to see who picked it up. If there were only a few complaints, they would immediately issue a credit to those particular customers and keep the increased prices for the rest. If they were inundated with complaints, they would reverse it. He told me that so far he had only issued three credit notes! So from his point of view it was a highly successful price increase that had put a substantial amount of money into his business. How often have companies done that to you, because you weren't paying attention? Have you been paying an increased price without realising it?

Controlling staff numbers and related costs

It is very easy to increase your staff numbers, but very difficult to cut back. This is an area that you need to think about very carefully, particularly in a small business. It's important for you to look very critically at how many people you require, while bearing in mind that at some point in the future you may need to reduce your staffing levels.

It's all too easy for people not involved in your business to tell you that you have too many staff and you need to reduce your headcount. But they don't know them all personally like you do. You may have known them for many years, live near them and know them socially, too. If you were the director of a large company, and didn't know them all personally, then you could look at it as if it were a mathematical problem. It would be simple: you have too many staff, you make some redundant, the figures will now balance. With that kind of distance between you, they'll be simply names on a piece of paper, not people you see for eight hours every day.

For small business owners, however, it's just not as easy as that. Some of your employees may have been with you for years – they may even be friends or family members. What is easier, though, is nipping this problem in the bud: do *not* take on any staff unless you have a solid business case for it. Can you say exactly how taking on that extra person or people will help you achieve your goal? If not, don't do it.

One of the easiest and least painful ways to reduce staff is to institute a policy of not replacing anyone who leaves. If someone moves on to pastures new, take it as an opportunity to check whether reorganising the business could save you the job of finding a replacement. You must, however, be ready to take someone on if the situation demands it: if you redistribute the leaver's tasks to such an extent that your other staff become overworked, dispirited and stressed, you run the risk of even more of them leaving and incurring recruitment costs. It's a delicate balance and one that you must consider carefully. Also, make sure that safety levels are not compromised: this affects some industries more than others, of course, but you must be 100% sure that you have enough staff to maintain proper checks and procedures.

Outsourcing

Once you start looking at staff levels, the next step is to look at your whole business and ask yourself whether all jobs need to be carried out on-site. Obviously your core business has to be operated in-house, but do you really need a bookkeeper on the premises? Could you engage a company to look after that function, or even look for a bookkeeper working from home? Subcontracting a job won't necessarily be very expensive, so check out some figures before you dismiss the idea out of hand.

I only got into my other life as the leader of a council to convince myself that politicians could reduce taxes while delivering better services, and I proved it to myself. During the four years I led the council:

- staff numbers were reduced by 40%
- the council's reserves doubled
- council tax went *down*, not up!

Subcontracting out services helped make many of these savings. For example, we sold off the works department, who did all the council's manual building work, because when you employ a subcontractor, if that specific job isn't being done correctly, you don't pay them. They soon sort it out because they need it in their cash flow.

What happens if the council uses its own employees to do that same job and it isn't done correctly? Those employees are given a verbal warning. If it still isn't done, a written warning is given, then the unions gets involved and it drags on and on. Meanwhile the costs for the job keep rising while, all the time, the job itself isn't being done. If you subcontract, the job gets done or they don't get paid – no argument.

There is a big proviso regarding this, of course. The contract between you and your subcontractor must be extremely clear about exactly what the job is and what the contractor is being paid to do. Spend as much time as you need to get this right;

many don't bother and end up being penalised severely, as in the case of Railtrack. When railways were privatised, poorly written contracts allowed companies to make profits out of properties but didn't define correctly the level of track maintenance required. This had dramatic results, including some horrific – and avoidable – accidents. For small businesses, the risks are normally (and thankfully) much smaller, but the principle is still valid.

Contracting out jobs is often popular with small businesses because it is a way of getting work done without having to fill in the myriad forms needed when businesses take on full-time staff. There are several benefits to this option, all of which reduce your costs and free you to concentrate on making money:

1. You only pay for the work done.
2. You get enormous flexibility as you only pay people when they are working.
3. You don't have the human resources responsibilities.
4. You have fewer forms to fill in.

Saving money in this way is great, of course, but don't let the extra money you now have to work with distract you from your important goal of reducing expenditure. When things go well, there's a danger that you will start feeling invincible and shift your focus from surviving day to day to thinking of your legacy and the big company you could build. This is when you become tempted to add staff. It's important to celebrate good news, but you must remember that as quickly as the money is pouring in, it can just as quickly stop. Make sure you save for a rainy day.

Also remember that even though there is lots of money flowing into the company, there is also lots of money going *out* to the creditors. You can't spend the whole lot! This is where your cash-flow chart comes into play again. Be strict with yourself and keep it up to date so that you know where every penny is going. You may be feeling a little more relaxed when things are going well, but don't let that mean that you splash out on items that you simply can't justify as a legitimate business expense. Will buying that new widget help you reach your business goal? No? Leave it.

15
STAFF: A WARNING

Your business is expanding. Your days are getting busier and you're spending more and more time at work. People may suggest that you need an assistant, so that you can focus on growing the business rather than admin and other time-consuming tasks that detract from your company's main purpose.

After a while, your PA explains that he is so busy that he needs an assistant himself and, because you're pleased with his work, you recruit one. This secretary finds that she is so busy that she doesn't have time to make the coffee, and so she asks your PA for an assistant, who naturally recommends that you take on an assistant for his secretary! Suddenly you have employed four extra people. They all need paying and, being individuals, have lives of their own with problems that need to be dealt with.

As your business becomes increasingly successful, this starts happening in all departments of your company. If you're not careful, staff inflation will get out of control. New employees are being taken on left, right and centre, and no single area of the business will be exempt. You will start asking yourself who you are working for – your staff, in order to pay their wages, or yourself? The answer will be your staff!

You now find that you are employing so many people that you need a specialist HR department to look after all them and to fill in the myriad government forms that multiply out of all proportion to the number of staff you employ. HR stands for Human Resources, which means, you've guessed it, more people! They will then tell you, in the nicest possible way, that your staff must have health and safety training, to meet the regulations. So, before you know it you have employed a safety officer. And so it goes on. Staff inflation in your company is growing and growing, and you can't seem to stop it.

While growing your company may well be something you want to do, each time that a new job is suggested, ask the Lindbergh question: 'Is this job being created for my comfort or to help me reach my goal?'

As we saw in Chapter 14, reducing expenses is essential in a cash-flow crisis. If you're in a very bad way, the quickest and most obvious way to do this is to cut down on staff numbers. But scruples aside, employment legislation means that shedding jobs is actually quite difficult. In fact, it seems that the only people you can release are those who generate the most income for the business – your sales team!

So they are the ones who must go, leaving you with an even bigger problem, as you are now left with a disproportionate number of admin staff, leaving the remaining income-generating employees to produce even more income in a slump, just to stand still!

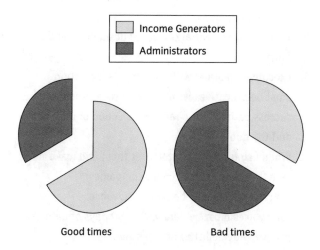

Good times   Bad times

The above pie charts show the problem.

The public sector provides many examples of what happens when bureaucracy takes over: projects are nearly always late and over budget. The most famous of recent years was the Millennium Dome. Far too late in the day, the government brought in a business troubleshooter, David James, to sort the mess out. He analysed the situation and then suggested a set of rules for governments to follow when setting up a major project in the public sector. They're actually pretty useful for any organisation taking on a major public challenge:

1. A major accountancy firm should control all key financial functions.
2. There must be central control of design and audit functions.
3. Executives charged with running the operation must be executives with a proven track record of success, rather than a random selection of the great and the good.
4. When using subcontractors, vet them and make sure that they are legitimate companies.
5. No cash should ever be paid in advance.
6. All invoices must be paid within 30 days of date of invoice, provided they are on schedule.
7. All cash-flow forecasts must be validated by independent external auditors.
8. Funding should be in place in advance, on a rolling four-week programme, before the cash needs to be spent.
9. An asset register should be set up and maintained to avoid arguments about the ownership of assets, and justify the success of the venture.

Very obvious and sensible points, you might think, and you'd be right. The fact that they were ignored until David James stepped in, though, shows how easy it is to get carried away when getting involved in a major or prestigious project. Bear these guidelines in mind if your business ever takes part in one.

The new Wembley Stadium is another major project that went wrong, and another one where the contract was written badly. The builders, Multiplex, agreed a finishing date for the new stadium and agreed to pay a penalty fee for each day they were late in completing the work. It sounds as though the Football Association did a good deal there, but they didn't. Multiplex added – and the FA agreed to – a cap on the late penalty fee. The building of the stadium ran so far behind schedule that they reached the cap and then had no further incentive to complete the job quickly, so the delay went on and on.

A great many companies move to the next stage of their development without sitting down to spend time planning that expansion. As ever, planning is crucial to success.

16
REDUCING YOUR COST OF SALES FIGURE

So far we've only looked at the expenses component of the 'daily cash out figure'. It's now time to turn our attention to the most important component of that: cost of sales.

As the name suggests, the cost of sales is literally that: the cost of producing whatever it is that you sell. Even if you offer a service to customers rather than a physical product, it still costs you money to create that service – never forget that your own time costs money. Whatever you sell, to improve your cash management you must always be looking for ways to reduce that cost of sale.

Until recently, I always used to look enviously at those people who were able to sell a product with an incredibly low cost of sale, as well as those guys in consultancy who were simply selling their time and therefore had no cost of sale. They had it made, or so I thought. That was until I ran a business where the cost of sale was less than 20% of the selling price. I was sure that this had to be easy, working with a gross profit margin of 80%, a figure I could only dream about in my previous businesses. But I soon learned that it wasn't easy and that the problems were exactly the same. We still need to reach a minimum level of sales. The cash still has to come through the door and there are still creditors to pay.

More importantly, at this profit margin, a 10% reduction in our cost of sale has less effect than a similar 10% saving in the computer industry, where we were working with gross profit margins of around 20%. When I was selling computers, a reduction in our cost of sales produced a noticeable increase in profit and cash, whereas at 80% it doesn't.

Philip Green can illustrate this concept for us. According to both the *Sunday Times* and the *Sunday Business*, when he bought BHS there was over £300 million of outstanding stock on order, and he learnt that one long-standing supplier was about to deliver £6 million of that stock. Philip Green called him and asked that before he delivered it, he should bring a sample of each item on the order to his boardroom and hang it up on the racks around the room. Philip Green then examined each item in minute detail.

When he had finished, he turned round to the supplier and said, 'Right, we're going to buy it all over again.'

The supplier replied, 'What do you mean? You've already bought it.'

It is said that he then replied, 'Yeah, but just for a bit of fun let's buy it all again.' He inspected each item again and then put forward an offer that the supplier simply couldn't believe.

He said, 'Look, this is where I think we are. You deliver your £6 million of goods. You get a cheque and don't come back. Or let's get in the real world and help me understand why I would pay £9 for an item that I can buy for £4'.

They then went through the order item by item, which meant that for each £1 reduction he got, he was putting £1 multiplied by the number of those units he sold straight into his bank account. He didn't need to increase sales; he simply had to reduce the amount he was paying for his goods, which is exactly what he did.

The reason Sir Philip got away with this was that he convinced his supplier that if he didn't accept the deal he would get no more orders, but if he did go for it,

> the growth of the business would mean that the supplier would end up with a lot more orders.

If you practise this principle regularly, you'll find you'll make massive savings along the way.

Saving money online

Advances in technology have given us new and interesting ways to reduce our cost of sales. The Internet in particular has changed the format of many new and existing companies by opening up many new ways to save.

In the late 1990s and early 2000s, people flocked to download music free from websites such as Napster. As the downloaders weren't paying for this music, copyright laws were being broken: the writers of those songs, the performers and their record companies were not being paid for their work. This led to a slump in the shares of the major record companies as everyone wondered how the record industry could survive, and, even more worryingly, why people should write songs if they weren't going to be paid for their efforts.

Then along came Apple with the iPod. Apple allowed people to download songs at very low prices – no more freebies. As Apple were charging a relatively small sum, however, people were prepared to pay to use their service and began to download songs legally. Apple signed agreements with all the major record companies and there was some speculation about why the companies agreed to such low figures.

Why? Because it was good cash management. What is being downloaded from the Internet is a song, an inanimate object. It isn't a physical object like a CD, which means that the record companies don't have to manufacture it. For them, their only cost of sale is the royalty fee, which is paid as a percentage of the sale price. The result is that suddenly the percentage of gross profit on music downloaded from the Internet has rocketed.

Now, if as a result of the low price many more people download the songs, this could drive the record companies' profits up. That is exactly what is happening. The number of music downloads are doing just that: they are growing at a galactic rate to stratospheric numbers, so much so that they are now included in the weekly record charts. As a result, the profits from EMI and the other record companies have started rising again.

This is just one example of how the Internet has changed business. It has allowed a large number of businesses to substantially reduce their cost of sale, and, let's be honest, that's what ultimately decides whether the company lives or dies. See it as the biggest library in the world: you can find out any price from any company with an online presence around the globe. For small business owners, it means that you have another tool to keep you in touch with the market and make certain that you are buying at the right price. So use it. You don't have to buy anything there and then if you don't want to, but armed with that information you are in a better position to negotiate your future deals.

As part of the preparation for starting up your business, you will have calculated very carefully your cost of sale and made sure that you've paid the best price available. Don't let this slide once the business is up and running: keep checking those costs regularly. Always look to see if there is a better way of doing business. If you stop checking and the market moves forward or it becomes cheaper to manufacture – and, therefore, buy – from a different country or supplier, you'll lose out and ultimately go under if you don't take advantage.

If you're buying to resell, once you're in the market and trading you must constantly look for better deals. Every time you hear of one, chase it. Make certain that, as your volume grows, you renegotiate with your suppliers. As you are a bigger customer, your suppliers should give you a better price or you can look elsewhere, reasonably confident that some-one else can be more competitive.

You must ask, though. Your suppliers won't automatically give you a better discount.

As your business grows, you'll start to be contacted by your suppliers' competitors; you're now a bigger and more tempting prospective customer. Contact of this type helps you keep in touch with the market, and is another way of making sure that you're getting the best possible price and that you're well equipped with information when you need to negotiate. These companies will be after your business, hoping to persuade you to buy from them. So, you should always see them and always keep an open mind. You don't have to buy from them today, but keep them in mind because, at some point in the future, you may need to find another supplier quickly because you have been let down.

This is why those companies trying to sell you goods are such essential tools as you build up a database of suppliers, making certain that you have the best prices and keeping you informed of what is happening in the marketplace.

Some time ago I worked for an office equipment supplier in Oxfordshire, and my boss, formerly the salesman covering one particular town, told me that he always kept calling on companies whether they would buy from him or not, because one day they might be in trouble and need a new supplier. He wanted to be that supplier. He then told me how it paid off. The biggest organisation in the town was the county council offices, who bought through their central purchasing department. For more than three years he visited the purchasing department on a weekly basis. Everyone knew him in the office and was always very friendly to him, but he never got even a sniff of an order.

Then one day he walked into the office, to a tremendous reception. They were expecting him. He was immediately taken into the top man's office. He had never even met him before that day. The top man then explained that they had a problem: some of the purchasing staff had been taking back-handers from several of their suppliers. They had been sacked and the suppliers blacklisted. The problem now was that they didn't know who to buy their office equipment from, as they had had a policy of not talking to salespeople. In spite of this policy, they did know him, because he kept calling. They were desperate for some stationery, and so they gave him a massive order! He had no competition as they had no time to go out to tender. He kept that account for many years after that.

The point is this: if companies don't talk to salespeople and stop getting mailshots and competitive information, how do they keep in touch with market prices? How do they learn what is out there? And how do they know what their competitors are doing?

I find it depressing that so many companies don't want to talk to salespeople. They subscribe to lists such as the Telephone Preference List, the Fax Preference List and the Mail Preference List to make certain that they don't receive 'junk mail'. I understand completely how unsolicited mail can drive you mad, especially when you get home from work to find the letterbox clogged up with random takeaway menus and other such wastes of paper, but I believe that there is merit in looking at work-related mailshots. Believe it or not, there *are* some benefits. For example, some time ago a computer company used to send out a fax each week giving the latest prices for computer chips and other components. Then along came the Fax Preference Service, set up by the government, and it became an offence to send faxes to people on the FPS list. It was an offence that could result in a fine of £5,000. Over the next few months the list halved, and I still wonder why all those companies who put themselves on to the FPS list didn't want to know what the best price for chips was.

I understand how frustrating it can be to find yourself bombarded with unsolicited mail at home, and it is totally wrong to send spam faxes or emails to private houses and individuals. There may be some benefits in a commercial environment, however. If you don't have the time to keep up with everything, faxes, emails and direct mailshots are a useful way to learn what is in the market. For example, recently we took a stand at a trade show. Our first decision was whether to take out a basic 'shell' stand and stick up a few posters, or put together something more striking. We made some enquiries and decided a special stand was way out of our league, so decided to put aside some money and see what we could do ourselves. That was our plan, at least, but we found that once we had booked the exhibition space, we were inundated with mailshots, faxes and emails from companies offering to build our stand. We learned from all this 'junk mail' that we *could* hire the sort of stand we wanted after all, and we would only have to pay for the graphics. If we had put ourselves on all these lists and refused to receive faxes, direct mail and email, we would never have known that we could achieve our dream within our budget. There are hundreds of similar examples, so make time every so often just to glance through all that junk mail – sometimes you'll find a gem.

Controlling manufacturing costs

If your business operates in the manufacturing industry, it's even more essential that you keep up to date with what is in the marketplace. Here again, mailshots of all kinds are essential tools to keep you informed. It appears to me that once you set up a production line and the line becomes operational, it develops a mind of its own that inevitably leads to extra costs. The trouble is that every increased cost, on its own, is justified every time. But when you look hard enough, you will find that *there is always a better way*.

I know a management consultant – let's call him Champagne Charlie (for reasons that will become clear). He specialises in manufacturing companies and claims he can go into any factory and reduce their production costs.

He regularly tells us about a visit he made to a company in the West Midlands. This company was situated at the end of one of the region's busiest high streets, and Charlie was in the managing director's office trying to convince him of the need for his services. He got so carried away that he inadvertently blurted out, 'anybody could walk into your factory and find ways to improve your efficiency'.

As you can imagine, the managing director was a bit put out, and challenged him. 'Charlie,' he said, 'look outside at all those people walking down the road. I'll pick one person, you go down and ask him to come into my factory and see if he can find ways to improve my production. If he does, I will give you a crate of champagne.' Charlie couldn't resist.

They both went over to the window, and Charlie nearly died. It was lunchtime and the road was packed! The managing director pointed out a short, fussy-looking man in a pair of slacks wandering along the road carrying a load of books. Charlie went down and approached him. He told him that he was in the office of this production company and explained the bet, asking if the gentleman would like to come into the factory and see if he could find anything that would improve its efficiency. The stranger was intrigued and agreed. He went in. Charlie introduced him to the managing director, who took him down to the shop floor and left him there. Charlie then sat in the outer office waiting, trying to convince himself that he hadn't been an idiot and regretting ever having made such a rash comment. Eventually the stranger came back and they both went back into the managing director's office. The stranger then explained that he was a teacher and therefore knew nothing about factories, having spent his life in schools. Charlie's heart sank. He then went on to explain that because he didn't understand such things he needed to ask a question.

His question was about why the machines were all laid out in the way they were, as he had noticed that some machinists, when they had finished a particular job, had to walk to the other end of the shop to hand it to the next machinist. He wanted to know why they weren't next to each other. There was a long pause and then the managing director said, 'Well, we didn't buy them all at once and we just put them in the next space. Do you know, we never even thought about it, we just put them in the next available space.'

Charlie got his job and a case of champagne, and has dined out on the story ever since!

Recently I met a management consultant, an expert in Japanese lean manufacturing techniques, which are geared towards making businesses more agile and productive. There's also a great emphasis on getting things right first time. This is basically the same as looking for 10% savings, except that the Japanese have been much more successful in finding savings and fitting them into the manufacturing process. The consultant told me how EasyJet had recently contracted his company to look at their maintenance procedures.

EasyJet only makes money while its aircraft are in the air. The longer they are standing still, the less money they make.

At regular periods every aircraft has to be taken out of service for regular maintenance, which takes 78 hours. He was contracted to see if this time could be reduced *without* compromising safety.

He and his team went into the hangar, watched and then questioned all the staff about everything that was done, asking simple questions like 'Why do you do that?' and 'Is there a better way?' It's amazing how much they learned about wastage simply by talking to the mechanics as they did their job. This, he told me, is where they find most of their savings. After a few weeks, they returned to EasyJet's boardroom. Using the information they had gleaned from the engineers in the servicing teams, they showed how the company could reduce the time each aircraft was out of service from 78 to just 38 hours – a phenomenal saving.

How did they do it? And where did the savings come from? Remember, the consultants' brief was to avoid compromising safety, and they stuck to this principle rigidly. Their solution was as follows: at a regular service the aircraft is basically taken to bits, each part checked and worn parts replaced. The aircraft is then re-assembled. The technicians told the consulting team that once an aircraft has been stripped down, it takes several hours to find the replacement parts before the plane can be put back together again. What the consultants did was put in place a first-class stock management system which allowed those replacement parts to be found more quickly. They didn't change the stripping down time or the rebuild time, just the bit in the middle, and by this simple change they reduced the maintenance time by nearly 50% without any risk at all to safety.

The lesson is to look continuously at your operation critically. *Never* think that you cannot make savings – you always can.

There are lots of other examples of profitable products that come from a suggestion from the shop floor. The popular Cadbury's Flake bar is one. A Flake is made up of the bits of chocolate that are left over from the other chocolate bars, and it came about because an enterprising employee suggested that they use these bits to make a bar. Thus the Flake was born: a high-volume product with a tiny development cost that has generated a lot of money. Could you apply the same criteria to your own business?

17

GOOD DEBT/ BAD DEBT

'Neither a borrower nor a lender be;
For loan oft loses both itself and friend,
And borrowing dulls the edge of husbandry.
This above all: to thine ownself be true,
And it must follow, as the night the day,
Thou canst not then be false to any man.'

Hamlet, Act I, Scene III

William Shakespeare has a lot to answer for. The first line of this speech has been quoted for centuries to warn hapless theatregoers of the dangers of debt. We hear a lot about debt and its attendant dangers in all walks of life, and Shakespeare's basic rule is a good one to follow as far as you can. In business, though, no enterprise can operate and grow without some form of debt.

We all have debts. They're practically unavoidable. For example, we're all in debt to utility companies until we pay them. It is the case nowadays that people either can't or won't wait to save up for something, and prefer to get hold of it right away by paying for it with a credit card or taking out a loan. Some people can't keep their personal debts under control, and this can have a massive negative impact on their lives. When you are starting or running a business, though, you will necessarily need to incur some debt as you stock your shop or develop the products you're going to sell. This doesn't mean, though, that you can throw caution to the wind. If you borrow for your business, make sure you stick to two key criteria:

- ■ know the difference between 'good' and 'bad' debt
- ■ aim to create only 'good' debt

Within reason, you can have as much good debt as you want, while you should aim to have as little bad debt as possible.

What's the difference between the two? Good debt is borrowed money that makes you more than the cost of borrowing it. For example, let's say you borrow some money to buy a building. You then let that building out. As long as the income generated by renting the building is more than the repayments on the loan, you have good debt. It is helping you to reach your goal.

A bad debt is borrowed money that is repaying previous debts, and is therefore not earning money. Taking out a loan to pay off a debt is bad debt in itself, as it is not earning you more money than it is costing you to borrow it. However, if as the result of this loan, your outgoings are reduced, allowing you to invest the savings in a way that will earn more than the cost of repaying the loan, it becomes a good debt.

If you have bad debt, you must constantly look for cheaper forms of borrowing that will bring down the cost of servicing it.

First, let's look at good debt, by assuming that we need to buy £1,000 worth of stock, which we then sell for £1,500. If we use £1,000 from our cash flow and then sell the stock for £1,500, we have made £500. This is a return of 50% on the original £1,000 of capital employed. If we borrow the whole £1,000, we still make £500. We may pay more interest – say £20 – but we still have our £1,000 to use for something else.

Most of us don't have the money to buy buildings out-right. Many of us don't even have the deposit, but 80% of us own our own home. In that house we have a chunk of equity, which is the difference between the value of the house and our mortgage. It could be possible to use that equity as security for a deposit on a second home with a buy-to-let mortgage. Provided that the rental on that property covers all the loan repayments, you have good debt. There is a flip-side, of course. If you use that extra money to go on a flash holiday rather than purchasing your buy-to-let, you're incurring bad debt, as the loan is not making you any money.

The key thing is not to get carried away. There are count-less examples of companies which, in boom times, use this formula to buy other companies without working out their figures correctly, which means that they haven't budgeted for quiet times. They work out how much they have to pay and base their interest calculations on the assumption that the boom times will continue indefinitely. When they stop (as boom times always do), sales drop. At the same time, interest rates always seem to rise and suddenly that good debt becomes a bad one as the monthly interest payments rise above the income being generated.

18
IMPROVING YOUR RELATIONSHIP WITH THE BANK

> Banks aren't always easy to deal with. Businesspeople can't live without them, so you need to find a way to live with them.

If you make life easy for the bank, it should follow that your own life gets easier too. Adopting this approach means attempting to look at things from the bank's point of view. To begin with, you need to understand that their agenda is different from yours. You'd think that you were both after the same thing – profits – and to an extent you are, but banks do it in two different ways.

First, they rely on individuals and businesses to deposit money with them, which they then lend out. They make their money on the small amount that remains with them – that is, the difference in interest rates. Naturally, to make a profit out of this small amount, they have to have an awful lot of money deposited with them. As the banks are such big concerns, they can do this, hence their size. To put this into perspective, Lloyds TSB Plc reported that in the financial year 2004–05, they were responsible for £175 billion of loans and advances. The small amount of that £175 billion that remained with them was only £5.671 billion. This sounds like a lot of money (and in normal situations it is!), but in fact it is only 3.24%, or 3.24 pence in every pound.

When they lend you money, they are making money, and therefore it follows that the more money they lend you, and the longer you have the loan, the greater the profits they can make for themselves. So why *is* it so difficult to get that loan?

Well, while it is true they only make their profits while lending, there is one massive proviso here: they only make a profit if you pay the loan back. If you can't, the bank has a colossal problem. For example, if High Street Bank Plc lends you £1,000 and you fail to pay them back, they haven't only got to make up for their lost profits, but they also have to replace the other 96.76% to reimburse the depositors who invested that money with them in the first place.

By extension, if the sum defaulted on was £10,000, the bank would have to make a further £297,176.80 to replace it all; if it were £100,000, they'd need to create a further profit of £2,971,768! You can see how massive the stakes are.

The absolute worst-case scenario for a bank is to be unable to make up the money that was lost as the result of an unpaid loan. The depositors would abandon them and they'd be flat broke in no time.

So that you really do understand your bank's problem, I want to take you into the director's suite of one of our major banks. Sit in the chief executive's chair and imagine that you've just got the job. You're running one of this country's largest banks. Yes, you are sitting in a big, panelled office at the end of a long, highly polished oak table that appears to stretch way into the distance. The walls are decorated with pictures of your predecessors, and around the table are deep leather chairs where your fellow directors are all seated. You've reached the top and you like it. You don't want to fail, and anyway the money's good and there will probably be a knighthood or damehood coming along soon.

You are in control of a business that employs over 70,000 people worldwide. They're all working for you, taking in money and lending it out. You are powerful. In fact, there aren't many more powerful positions in the business world. But there's a problem. One so great that it could finish you and send you tumbling all the way back to the bottom of the heap. And it could happen so easily.

Just imagine, for a moment, what would happen if just one of those 70,000 people is a rogue trader, who lends too much or lends to too many risky businesses? It can happen – remember Barings Bank. You could be in terrible trouble. Think about it. How can you possibly know what the manager in a tiny branch in Anytown is actually lending and, even more worrying, how can you possibly know whether or not he or she is putting the whole bank at risk with some reckless advances?

You can't. The bank is too big and there are too many people for you to personally vet them all, so how do you sleep at night?

There is only one way to be able to sleep soundly, and that is to put in place strict rules about the type of company your managers can lend to and the security that they can lend against. You must insist that everybody in the organisation has a copy of these rules, that they are fully trained in them, know how to implement them and abide by them no matter what. You have to make certain that whenever your people lend money, they do so against adequate security which, if necessary, can be sold off very easily. This is the only way to protect yourself and be able to sleep soundly.

When you talk of security you will want the safest and best form of security that, if things go wrong, enables you to get at least some of the money back. That security must be safe, it must be there when you need it, and it must be easy to convert into money. This means that you need the safest security in the world, and that is property. Why? Because property can't walk! This is why if you were sitting in the chief executive's office, you would make it as difficult as possible for your bankers to lend on anything that is not completely covered by security that can repay the loan, such as property.

Now I am going to bring you back to earth, take you into your local bank manager's office and put you on the other side of the desk. You're there because you need a loan. You need to persuade your bank manager that you are a good risk and that he or she should lend you money. (This is, of course, before the benefits of your new cash management regime have put you into the position where you are cash-rich and don't need an overdraft.)

Once your business has cash in the bank, you'll find that your bank manager wants you as a new best friend. Why? Because you are now a safe risk and the powers that be are happy to lend you money. This is why Phillip Green was able to raise nearly £10 billion from the banks in his recent attempt to buy Marks & Spencer. The banks knew he was a safe risk and that they'd be able to make a lot of money out of him.

So what do you do to persuade the bank manager to lend you money, knowing what you do about life at the top of the bank? First of all, obviously we must offer whatever security we have. If that isn't enough, use your business plan and cash-flow charts to show where the business is going. Then ask the bank manager if any shortfall can be covered by the government-backed Small Firms Loan Guarantee Scheme (SFLG).

This scheme was set up in the 1980s but is still going strong and is administered by the Department for Trade and Industry. Find out more about it via Business Link (**www.businesslink.gov.uk**) or the Small Business Service (**www.sbs.gov.uk**). If you meet its criteria and the bank manager will endorse the viability of your business idea, you can get a loan without security. Basically, the theory behind it is that small businesses have many good ideas that could be exploited if the banks would only lend them the money to develop these ideas, but small businesspeople usually don't have enough security of the type that the bank would accept. Therefore, the government decided that it would act as guarantor, provided that the banks felt that the proposal concerned was a viable business idea. So far, so good.

There is, of course, a catch. The problem came when the government said that it would not underwrite all the borrowing. The government's reasoning was very simple and, from its perspective, makes lots of sense. They reasoned that if they underwrote all the debt, the banks would move all their more dubious loans into the scheme and the government would end up picking up the tab. So to stop this they said that they would only guarantee 70% of the debt and the banks should take a risk on the remainder.

Now we hit a major problem. Let's go back to the boardroom and ask our new chief executive – that's you, remember – would you take that risk? The result is that now the scheme only works if you are prepared to give the bank some form of security to cover that remaining 30%, but you mustn't tell the government, as then they won't provide the extra guarantee, because they want the banks to take the risk.

This is why you need to have as good a relationship as possible with your bank manager. Keep him or her informed of what you're up to and see how he or she can help you out. It's always worth giving the Small Firms Loans Guarantee Scheme a go.

The figures I quoted earlier on the amount of profit the banks make on lending have come from the banks' accounts, and are a bit on the high side, as it was not possible to split the income from lending and that from their other income generator.

This other income generator is the reason that no matter how rich you get you will always need a bank. As you know, you can never be in business without using a bank. We all need them. How else could we clear cheques?

This is the second income-generating sector for our banks. They like this business and try to get as much of it as possible. The benefit for them is that it is far less risky; it is purely an administrative business. They simply match up pieces of paper with sums of money on them. It is a good, profitable business and one in which they can find lots of safe ways to add additional charges and make lots of money, and they do – just look at your bank statement!

Controlling bank charges

As you know, banks charge you for every transaction they carry out, however small. While we accept that they can't be avoided completely, you can take steps to minimise the amount you pay. For example:

- **Visits**. It's easy to control being charged for visiting the bank: only go to see your bank manager in person if it's essential – if you are hoping to borrow some money, say. If the manager invites you in for a meeting, ask whether the issue can be discussed over the phone. If it can't be, ask for the fee to be waived if at all possible.

- **Cheques**. Fewer people pay by cheque these days, but most businesses will have to pay them in at some point, and as your business becomes more successful, that number will grow. Most banks charge between 70p and £1.20 for each cheque you pay in, which doesn't sound like a lot, but it does add up. For example, if your average cheque value is £12 and you are paying a £1.20 charge per cheque, this means that you are giving 10% of your turnover to the bank! Even if your average cheque value is higher – £50, say – you're still giving the bank 2.4% of your turnover.

What can you do about it? Well, most banks offer free banking for the first year, and some even offer two years. It shows how profitable this side of banking is that they are so keen to attract your custom. Take advantage of these offers and at the end of the free period, renegotiate your charges. If you have no luck, try another bank.

■ **Move accounts if you need to**. As shown above, there's plenty of competition for your money, so don't be afraid to move on if you feel you're not getting the service you want. Shop around for a bank that is more competitive. It can be a hassle to keep changing regularly, though, so you need a more permanent solution: you need a deposit-taking bank that doesn't charge per cheque, such as Cater Allen (**www.caterallen.co.uk**).

The importance of negotiation

To increase your margins, and thereby increase the cash in your business, you must negotiate. There are several ways of doing this. Sometimes, if your turnover is large enough, you can negotiate a monthly fee for the bank to clear all your cheques. If your normal bank won't go with that, you could use a secondary deposit-taking bank, as mentioned above. Normally these banks limit the number of free cheques they will clear without charging, but if your business has a lot of them, they're happy to negotiate. These banks also allow you to write a small number of cheques, say 20 a month, without a charge. The beauty of such accounts is that they pay interest on the deposits, so you save on bank charges and also have the advantage of a small interest payment.

One of our companies gets a lot of small cheques, so we have opened an account with such a bank and successfully negotiated to clear our cheques for nothing, in return for a reduced interest rate. We see this as beneficial as we don't lose any of our turnover, and with our average cheque size being £40, this makes a substantial saving to our monthly expenditure.

Check your statements

Everyone makes mistakes, and banks are no exception. As part of your new cash management regime, you'll be looking at all your costs, and keeping an eye on all bank-related costs is no exception. To this end, always check your bank statements every time they arrive. If you find an error, contact the bank immediately: they will normally act quickly.

There is the true story of the customer who found that he had been overcharged by £18,000. When the bank were told, they admitted it, repaid the money and then actually asked him to take his account elsewhere! Worrying really, as it leads you to assume that they know they can't control their mistakes and therefore do not want customers who check their statements.

There is another story about a customer with several accounts at the same bank, some holding large sums of money and others in overdraft. The bank confirmed that all the account balances would be totalled together and interest, if the total was in overdraft, would be charged only on the total balance of all the accounts.

BANKCheck, a private consultancy, conducted an audit on the bank accounts and the results were frightening. It appeared that the bank had added the fee for equalising the accounts to the quarterly interest amount and then debited a single amount to the client's account under the heading of bank interest!

When the bank was asked about this fee, they said it was standard practice to charge a fee for this work. But the bank had not told the customer about this fee at any time, and on searching all the bank statements for the actual fee, it couldn't be found, even though the bank said it was charged on a quarterly basis.

Eventually, following a number of meetings, the bank finally admitted that the fee had been hidden in the interest charge and a refund of £135,000 was made to cover a three-year period!

On another occasion, a company with an overdraft facility of £100,000 was overcharged by £87,000 over a six-year period. The interest rate on their account was supposed to be 3% base rate, but the bank was charging almost 7.5% above base rate!

To do a rough check, **www.ChargeChecker.co.uk** gives the following advice:

1. Look closely at interest charges over as long a period as possible. Do any of the charges appear to be out of step without reason? Are you staying within the limits set by the bank?
2. Add up the statement balances in a high overdraft period, then multiply by the agreed percentage and divide by 36,500. The result should not be more than three-quarters of the amount charged. If it is, then further investigation is needed.

If you want to challenge the figures:

1. Make absolutely sure that the bank's statements are complete.
2. Gather together all correspondence to and from the bank.
3. If your business deals with a lot of cash, collect together all paying-in books so that the cleared and uncleared credits can be separated and then compared with the bank's credits.

4. Now find a cheque checking company such as Charge Checker (**www.chargechecker.co.uk**) or BANKCheck (**www.bankcheck.co.uk**).

So, we have established that banks make mistakes, try to cover them up and are reluctant to admit them, but businesses still can't operate without them. The best way to deal with your bank manager is the same way that you should deal with creditors: keep everyone informed. If you have agreed to supply any information to the bank by a certain date each month, make sure that you meet that date whatever you do. If you fail, they will assume the worst and could take drastic action.

The problem with dealing with banks is that they are so big that, unless you are negotiating for millions of pounds, you are dealing with managers who have little or no room for manoeuvre. They're often allowed only to lend you money if the right boxes are ticked in a set of spreadsheets and if you have enough security to cover the amount of requested borrowing. As mentioned earlier, this security has to be in the form of a property or negotiable securities. It is no use offering them stock, because stock is (to them) dead money.

Let the Internet help you

If you feel that you will not be using an overdraft – and once you start using the principles we've covered in this book, that shouldn't be far away – look for the bank that gives you the best interest on your current account. Many of the online banks can offer much better rates. Not all of them have business accounts at the moment, but it's likely that they soon will.

One other benefit of banking online is the ease with which you can check your accounts. Make it a habit to review them regularly: make a date in your diary to do it every Monday morning, say, or whenever works best for you. Checking your balance regularly means that not only can you pick up on potential problems much more quickly, but you can also reduce your costs and borrowing requirements at the same time. For example, you can see exactly when a cheque arrives and can therefore accurately calculate when you need to pay your own suppliers, confident in the knowledge that there will be money there to meet it.

18
ZERO-INTEREST BORROWING

Don't worry, your eyesight isn't failing. Borrowing at zero interest really is possible!

Most companies fund themselves through bank borrowing, mainly in the form of a bank overdraft. We all know how difficult it can be to secure one of these. There are other ways, though. The offers come through our front door on glossy leaflets every day. Yes, I'm talking about credit cards.

A brief but important word of warning

Please take great care with credit cards. If you manage them sensibly, they will give you free credit and may help you out of financial difficulty in the short term. If you take your eye off the ball, they are probably the most expensive form of credit available to you.

Whenever you go to the bank to get an overdraft or even to increase your current one, you'll probably encounter the following scenario:

1. The bank charges you an arrangement fee.
2. The bank manager then explains that she needs you to sign a personal guarantee. Oh, and by the way, she'll want the deeds to your house.
3. She'll then need to think about it and will get back to you in a few days.
4. Finally, when she does get back in touch, if she agrees to it, she'll insist that you give her figures on a regular basis in order that your progress can be monitored. Oh, and naturally charge you a bit more as they are doing this work for you!

So, in order to borrow money from a bank, you must:

- pay them to set it up
- wait for them to decide whether you are a good risk or not
- give up the protection of limited liability
- give them the deeds to your house
- agree to spend time putting together your figures that they never understand, until you have a bad month, when they always look at the negatives,

(never the positives), whereupon they threaten to take this overdraft away!

■ finally, pay a higher interest rate because – as they will invariably tell you – they are taking a special risk

Now contrast this with what comes through your letterbox when you get home. Regular mailshots from banks and credit-card companies, offering you loans and credit cards with from six to 15 months' free credit, confirmed in advance, with no questions asked. The irony is that they're all from the same banks who are asking you to jump through hoops: they own the credit-card companies.

Your business can benefit from credit cards if you proceed carefully:

1. Take out a new credit card with six months' free interest and put that money into your business, either by using it to buy necessary items or by depositing a credit card cheque into your business.

2. Make a note in your diary to find and open a new credit card offering six months' free credit in five months' time. Once you've been accepted, move your outstanding balance to the new card.

3. Cut up the first credit card *as soon as* your balance has been transferred. Do *not* keep it: you run the

risk of being tempted to use it again if you run into cash difficulties.

We can now loan that money to our business. Please remember that you *still* have personal liability, but:

- you have not had to pay a set-up charge
- you are paying no interest
- you don't have to spend time placating the bank manager
- you don't even have to have a special interview!

As a bonus, your bank manager now looks on you favourably as your account is always in credit.

Earlier in the chapter, we looked at the fact that if you do use credit cards for a time, one benefit is that you don't have to produce regular figures for your bank manager. It's vital, however, that you keep regular figures for yourself – you must know the real position your business is in. (Remember the guy or girl in the mirror.)

Why do you need to keep on top of things? Because the credit card companies that offer six months (or more) or more interest free do charge very high interest fees once that period comes to an end. They know that people will probably forget when their interest-free period finishes and that they'll accidentally end up paying the higher figure. To avoid this trap, you must keep a close eye on your cash-flow chart and know when you need to move to another credit card.

If you manage this carefully, you can build up your company on borrowed money without paying any interest charges at all. This is 'good' debt, which comes with an added bonus: you don't have to keep justifying yourself to the bank manager when you have a bad month.

Keep the rules in mind

You do, of course, have some obligations when you take out a credit card, the main one being that you must make certain that you pay at least the minimum every month *on time*. If you miss a payment even by just 24 hours, you'll end up in the 'credit penalty box'. Once you're there, the credit card company accelerate you to the worst interest rate immediately. Therefore, once you have decided to use this method of funding, it's time to be disciplined. Follow these credit card rules:

1. Set up a direct debit that pays off your monthly minimum payment.
2. Make a note in your diary to alert you six weeks before an offer ends. This is essential, or you will end up on the higher interest rate.
3. Apply for a new card one month before the offer ends. This allows enough time for you to get the new one in place.

4. Always transfer balances between cards. It is cheaper than using cash withdrawal or a credit card cheque (you'll usually be charged in both of these instances).

5. Again, cut up the card once you have paid back the balance. Do not keep it on the premises in case you're tempted to use it.

By using these rules we were able to borrow over £30,000 on a variety of credit cards. We didn't borrow it all at once, as it took time to build up the assets we were creating. The money only had to be invested gradually over a period of time. We were also fortunate in that our money requirements matched the growth in credit limits that we received whenever we moved to a new credit card.

Every week the *Sunday Times* runs an interview on the back page of its *Money* section about how successful people manage their funds. They always ask, 'what has been your best investment?' Some time ago they interviewed the composer Gordon Haskell, who enjoyed success in 2001 with the release of his ballad 'How Wonderful You Are', which was swiftly followed by the album *Harry's Bar*. His answer to this question was 'Paying for the production of my albums. *Harry's Bar* cost me £7,000 plus interest on my credit cards. In total I got back £700,000!'

We may not all be able to emulate this success, but remember that there is always the credit-card option!

The other side of the fence

Credit cards are much more useful to your business than merely as a simple form of borrowing. They are many people's preferred method of payment, especially when buying online.

For business owners, they are an absolute boon: in fact, if everybody paid you by credit card, life would be easy. Think how many debtor days it would put into your bank, without your having to spend time chasing.

If you don't accept credit cards, make it a priority to sort this out. The main benefits to you are:

1. Once you have an acceptance number from the credit card company, you know that you will be paid.
2. The money will then be in your bank account as cleared funds within three to five working days (depending on the bank you use).
3. You reduce your debtor weeks, as nobody seems to query the fact that when they pay by

credit card they are paying in advance or on collection.

4. It gives your overseas customers the protection of the credit card company, if, for example, you fail to deliver the goods. At the same time, you benefit from knowing that you have been paid. It is a much simpler form of overseas payment than letters of credit.

5. You can extend your credit by 30 days simply by paying your supplier on 60 days with the company credit card.

6. You can pay for overseas orders with them; your supplier then has a guarantee of payment while UK credit card laws protect you if the goods don't arrive as agreed.

At the same time, there are many benefits to your customer. For example:

1. They get a further 30 days' free credit.
2. It doesn't affect their overdraft.
3. They too have the protection of the credit card company if you fail to deliver.

20
HAVE YOU EVER HEARD OF . . .?

The Government Procurement Card (GPC)?

This is a credit card that is available for use by all public sector organisations, allowing them to pay for goods immediately. In other words, it is the government's credit card. Some years ago the National Audit Office found that when the Ministry of Defence went out to buy an item of a very low value, such as a padlock costing 80p, the cost of requisitioning, obtaining quotes, issuing a purchase order and so on came to £90! They had to find another way, and that other way was the GPC. The Audit Office like it because they say that it frees up valuable resources that can then be used elsewhere.

In theory, the GPC can be used for all purchases where you or I would use a credit card. In broad strokes:

- It is issued to selected members of staff, giving them the authority to buy low-value goods and services, such as stationery (in some circumstances, the GPC can be used to buy much more expensive items – costing up to tens of thousands of pounds – but in the main, expenditures tend to be relatively small).
- It cuts out the need for purchase orders, thereby eliminating the paperwork connected with raising such orders.
- At the end of each month, the card operator sends in a single invoice with all that month's expenditure laid out.
- Each cardholder has his or her own individual spending limit.
- Card limits can be changed very simply.

As you can see, it functions as a credit card and has all the benefits of such a card – exactly the benefits a business gets from using credit cards.

How does it work?

- Cardholders place orders with organisations that accept Visa.
- Orders can be made online, by fax or over the phone.

- Cardholders keep a record of all transactions, allowing them to monitor their expenditure.
- Once the card has been accepted, the goods can be delivered to the cardholder or the designated delivery point.
- Each cardholder receives his or her own monthly statement.
- At the end of the month, the finance department of the organisation using the card receives a consolidated statement showing the total expenditure for the month, itemised across individual cards.

It is exactly the same system as if you were to issue credit cards to your staff. You would benefit by delegating the buying authority to another employee, while still being able to monitor that expenditure through the monthly credit card bill. If your employee spent above their limit, you would be able to sort it out directly with that person.

The GPC has one other enormous benefit to small business owners. Historically, selling to the public sector is a nightmare. You have to submit tenders, then, once you win one, you have to find a way to get paid within a reasonable time. Government doesn't purposely delay payments, but it is such a large and cumbersome beast that this often ends up being the result. If you are approached by a government department asking to pay by GPC, jump at the opportunity. Provided that you have a credit card facility, the money will be in your bank account within four days, and you don't even have to chase the accounts department to get it; it comes in automatically. It makes dealing with the public sector so much easier.

It is very interesting to see which public bodies are currently using them and their reasons. For example, the Metropolitan Police use them to book flights for policemen. In 2005, they required more than 6,000 flights to send police officers on overseas duties, many of them on very short notice – they are responding either to a request from the Foreign Office or to an emergency somewhere in the world. When this happens, it can mean that they need to book flights and hotels in a matter of hours, and they have found that since they started using the card, they have been able to book flights online almost immediately.

The Scottish Executive did a creditors' analysis, which showed that they had made 60,000 low-value ad hoc purchases and payments for less than £1,000. By moving to a Government Procurement Card they made enormous savings in administrative costs.

There are many more examples of government departments using the GPC, so if your business sells to public bodies, make it clear to them that you will accept it. Everyone will benefit!

21

DISCIPLINE

I was sitting in my office one day when the phone rang. The voice at the other end sounded desperate. He introduced himself as Chris, and he wanted our help. Chris explained that he had a highly profitable company but no money in the bank; it was all owed to him. He asked if we could come in and show his staff how to get his debtors to pay up at last.

We arrived and learned that the company had a turnover of £800,000 with outstanding debtors of £300,000, which equated to 19.5 weeks. That's nearly five months! We then saw their terms of trade. They were 'payment in advance unless credit terms had been agreed'! They were in a trade where, traditionally, you got paid in advance, but from the figures it was clear that they were giving everyone credit. Why was this happening?

Well, they had a highly motivated sales team to whom the weekly sales figure was paramount. All the correct rules were in place, but if the team got close to the end of the week and hadn't yet beaten their target, they were breaking them and offering credit to get as many sales as they could. Their commitment was never in question, but discipline had gone out of the window. The result? A highly profitable company on paper, but one with nothing in the bank; credit was being given to all and sundry, irrespective of their credit history, just to get the orders in.

You'll never be able to manage your cash flow effectively if you have no discipline. You can have as many rules as you like, but if you don't stick to them, you won't get anywhere. For example, in this particular case it was reasonably simple to find a way to make certain that every order was paid for in advance.

So how could the situation be turned round? We used the fact that the sales team was so focused. As there was no point in damaging that enthusiasm by imposing a strict payment-with-order system, we had to use both the carrot and the stick. To begin, we made it clear that they had to stick to the rules, but at the same time we gave them an additional 2% commission for taking credit-card payment when they won an order. As the team could see more money coming in, they rose to the challenge and pretty soon the company was getting its cash sorted out and moving forward. It was cash-rich very quickly. In fact, within three days the turnaround was obvious to everyone.

This story sums up the essence of this book in a way. It's easy to read through and say 'oh, we do X', and 'of course we do Y'. But you must actually *do* something about a difficult situation, not just pay lip service to potential solutions. As a test, ask a trusted friend to place a 'dummy' order with your company and see whether the 'unbreakable' rules you have in place are holding up as well as you think they are.

Set the tone

When you run your own business, it's important that you set a good example. It won't help your staff if they see or hear you making deals or offers that you've explicitly told them not to make. Empower them to help you. Make it clear to everyone on the sales team that even if a senior person in the business asks them to break a rule of sale, they have your complete backing to say 'no'. Whether you tell them in meetings, by e-mail, on your intranet or in your company newsletter, make sure that everyone is aware of how far they can – and can't – go.

As ever, keep in touch. I've always found that when I have a problem with anyone, it is better to talk to them as soon as possible so that I can address the issue at an early stage. Discipline yourself to do just that. If you put it off, it's likely that the problem will build up in your own mind and you'll start imagining what the other person may be up to; on the other side of the fence, the person you need to speak to will be worrying about what *you're* going to do. By the time you meet, you're already at an impasse.

To illustrate, we often tell new salespeople the following story of a small tenant farmer. Let's call him Bob Jones. Bob had just got married and together with his wife, Blodwen, was trying to make a go of a small tenant farm on the hills of Wales. They had a few fields where they were rearing sheep. All their rams died suddenly and they needed help, but couldn't afford to buy new ones on their own.

Blodwen suggested that Bob go and talk to the owner of their neighbouring farm and see if he could help them. Bob was reluctant to do this, because their neighbouring farmer was rich and obviously successful and Bob felt inferior. Blodwen told Bob that this attitude was stupid and sent him off to see Mr Barrington-Evans, their wealthy neighbour.

Bob left the farm and started out crossing the first field. As he did so he thought about his mission and decided that of course it would work – people like to help others. He got to the second field and started thinking about Mr Barrington-Evans. He always seemed so superior. They were neighbours, but had never even spoken. Would this man really help him?

By now, Bob had made it across all the fields and was walking up a wide drive to an imposing country house. (Well, in his mind it had grown into a massive stately home.) He'd come to the conclusion that his neighbour was a superior, stuck-up, upper-class twit, and decided that he wasn't going to take any lip from him.

Bob finally reached the front door, rang the bell and waited. By now it wasn't fear that gripped him, it was fury at this man. The door was opened by a large, round, chubby man with a friendly face, who said, 'Oh hello, you're the chap from that hill farm, aren't you?'

To which Bob replied, 'Yes, and I won't take any lip from you and I don't want to borrow any rams anyway!' Then he turned around and walked away.

The moral? Never let your imagination get the better of you. You start imagining the worst and never get beyond that.

Build networks of trusted colleagues and friends – it's always good to know people who you know will tell you the unvarnished truth – and go out of your way to find new contacts, too. You never know when you might need their help and you could also assist them in useful ways too.

Be strict with yourself and develop some good habits. The first of these is updating your cash-flow chart. Get into the habit of amending it every time money comes in, every time it goes out or whenever you raise an invoice. I recommend doing it first thing in the morning, but if another time works better for you, fine. Just make sure it gets done. It won't take you long to get used to it and will be well worth it.

Also, make sure that your accounts team (if you have one) get into the habit of chasing debts. They should ring the people invoiced a week earlier to make sure that everything is progressing smoothly. If a problem surfaces, you can take action to sort it out promptly. You'll find that your debtor days will keep coming down while your bank balance will keep going up. Consistency is the key here: if you only chase occasionally, you won't enjoy long-term success.

22
THINK CASH!

Small and medium-sized businesses are essential to a thriving economy. Most innovation comes from small companies: look at Microsoft, for example. Thirty years ago it was a tiny, two-man company; now, it is one of the biggest in the world. Vodafone, the largest telecoms company, just didn't exist. Without small companies striving to grow and develop, our vibrant economy would die and we would still be back in the age of the horse and cart.

However, small business owners often don't get the recognition they deserve. It take a lot of courage to start up your own company, but if things don't work out (as can happen for a variety of reasons), entrepreneurs are often made to feel like pariahs. To survive in this context, we need help, and sometimes we need to look outside our normal circle of contacts, which is why I wrote this book.

Today, it can seem as though government pays lip service to the small business sector, having set up organisations such as Business Link. Some do produce real results, but far too many of them don't have the resources to make a real difference. In fact, I would say that businesses succeed *despite* the barriers put up against them by central government.

I was the leader of a council in Warwickshire for some time. After I retired, I set up a new business and naturally went to Business Link for a grant. When I arrived for my interview, I was surprised to find that the interview panel was made up not of experienced businesspeople, but of officers from my old council! They knew nothing about business. I had spent the previous four years trying to instil some business understanding in them even though, on paper, they all had the right qualifications. Needless to say, I didn't get the grant.

There is a sequel to this story. A couple of years later I was invited by Business Link to a meeting. The chairman of the meeting explained that the attendees had been invited because we had all applied for a grant and had our application turned down, but our businesses had survived. He had been given the task of finding out why we had been successful, while why those companies that had been awarded grants had failed. It was an interesting meeting, but changed nothing.

I have had to develop my own way to survive in business and make it work. My aim has been to distil those lessons in a way that will help as many small business owners as possible.

I also started to run courses based on the themes covered in the book, and these courses allow me and my colleague to go into companies and help other people who have been in the position I was. Many of these people are mentioned in the preceding chapters and they've benefited from the cash-management principles I believe in. If this book has helped you just a little, and some of the ideas and tips have made you more money than the book cost you, I have succeeded.

As I said at the beginning, this book has been written to show the benefits to be gained from the single most important route to profit, the simple principle of managing your cash effectively. Use the techniques covered and you'll start to look at your business differently. Eventually, it'll mean that you get fewer difficult phone calls from your bank manager, which in turn will give you more time to concentrate on making money – oh, and, of course, filling in all those new forms the government sends us!

Good luck!

INDEX